Convicted
But Innocent

Convicted *But* Innocent

Wrongful Conviction and Public Policy

C. RONALD HUFF
ARYE RATTNER
EDWARD SAGARIN

I.C.C. LIBRARY

SAGE Publications
International Educational and Professional Publisher
Thousand Oaks   London   New Delhi

For information address:

 SAGE Publications, Inc.
2455 Teller Road
Thousand Oaks, California 91320
E-mail: order@sagepub.com

SAGE Publications Ltd.
6 Bonhill Street
London EC2A 4PU
United Kingdom

SAGE Publications India Pvt. Ltd.
M-32 Market
Greater Kailash I
New Delhi 110 048 India

Printed in the United States of America

Library of Congress Cataloging-in-Publication Data

Huff, C. Ronald.
    Convicted but innocent: Wrongful conviction and public policy /
authors, C. Ronald Huff, Arye Rattner, Edward Sagarin.
       p. cm.
    Includes bibliographical references and index.
    ISBN 0-8039-5952-4 (cloth: acid-free paper).
    ISBN 0-8039-5953-2 (pbk.: acid-free paper).
    1. Judicial error—United States. 2. False imprisonment—United States
    3. Criminal justice, Administration of—United States.
    I. Rattner, Arye. II. Sagarin, Edward, 1913–1986. III. Title.
    KF9756.H84   1996
    364.1'092'273—dc20   95-41748

This book is printed on acid-free paper.

96 97 98 99 10 9 8 7 6 5 4 3 2 1

Sage Project Editor: Christina Hill

This book is dedicated to the memory of our friend and colleague, Professor Edward Sagarin, whose ideas and encouragement contributed greatly to this book and to our lives; and to the convicted innocents, whose cause he championed.

C.R.H.
A.R.

Contents

Foreword

Of the many troubled social institutions in American life—including public education, welfare, health, and the family—none is in greater difficulty than the criminal justice system. Many billions of federal dollars have been spent on criminal justice agencies and programs since the introduction of the Law Enforcement Assistance Administration in the late 1960s in the "war on crime" stemming from persistent public pressure for greater personal safety. Astronomic sums have been allocated to upgrade law enforcement equipment; to go on-line in this computer age so that law enforcement agencies can more efficiently collect, record, maintain, and share information; to improve forensic science; to recruit and train additional qualified personnel (more than 100,000 new police officers alone in the latest crime bill, 1994-1995); to reduce racial, gender, and ethnic biases in the system; to speed up the criminal justice process; to rewrite the criminal codes and impose draconian sentences on those convicted of drug offenses; to revive the death penalty; to move toward definite (fixed) sentences, of longer duration; and to upgrade the efficiency and effectiveness of the various criminal justice subsystems, including the police, prosecution, courts, and corrections.

Much, much more needs to be done in nearly every facet of the criminal justice enterprise to modernize policing, prosecution, the judicial arm, and the corrections subsystems, including probation, parole, and adult and juvenile prisons and training schools, and to improve efficiency. The corrections system is currently so large that the adult prison system employs more people than any other agency in state government. Significantly, the cost of supporting the swollen criminal justice enterprise is now about half of the total expenditures of large metropolitan communities, especially in highly urban counties. In every legislative session, more criminal justice bills are introduced, and usually left to die without consideration, than bills in any other substantive area. The vastness of the investment in money, personnel, and physical facilities is neither known nor generally understood by the general public, who continue to rank "the crime problem" among their top three concerns—usually as number one.

The criminal justice system has launched massive and costly efforts, especially in the never-ending "war on drugs," to prevent and control crime; to incapacitate repeat and dangerous offenders; to neutralize urban street gangs in large and small cities and in the prisons; to reduce the incidence of DUI (driving under the influence of alcohol or drugs); to do something about sex offenders, white-collar criminals, and spouse abusers. Efforts have also been made to rehabilitate offenders through K-12 and sometimes postsecondary education programs in prison, vocational training, work, social skills training, counseling, and all the rest. Still, the record remains bleak and the public dubious about the outcome of these efforts and, more generally, of the "war on crime." It is, of course, true that official *Uniform Crime Reports* data show that crime peaked in the 1970s, held steady during the first half of the 1980s, and has declined in the past 10 years. The number of all reported "index crimes"—murder and nonnegligent manslaughter, rape, robbery, aggravated assault, burglary, larceny-theft, auto theft, and arson—fell sharply in 1994 and even more sharply in the first half of 1995. Corroboration of this welcome trend is to be found in victimization studies conducted by the Census Bureau and by academic researchers. For some years now, households and business establishments have reported significant declines in the most common personal and property crimes.

At the same time, incarceration rates (adult and juvenile prison and jail populations) have been increasing, with no sign yet that they have begun to level off. Nationally, there are now more than 1 million prison inmates—more than 100,000 in California alone, and Texas and Florida will approach this number before long. In Ohio, as in many other jurisdictions, the number of prisoners has quadrupled since 1970 and doubled since 1980. Where there were once 7 Ohio adult institutions holding 7,700 inmates (1973), at midyear in 1995 there were more than 43,000 convicts in 28 prisons. California's prison system used to take 4% of that state's budget; it now gets 8%—the additional 4% mostly from funds that could have been spent on education. In Ohio, as elsewhere, the increase in the penal population has occurred primarily because of the "war on drugs"; the legislative upgrade in sentences jumped the average time served in confinement in Ohio from 2.2 years to well over 4 years for inmates paroled in the 1980s and remained constant at 1.1 years for those released on definite sentences. Stricter enforcement of the conditions of parole has resulted in an unprecedented jump in parole violators returned to prisons. An assortment of other changes, including the tightening of the system leading to the incarceration of greater numbers of convicted felons and the shrinking in the proportion granted parole, when eligible, accounts for the rest of the increase. The number of lesser offenders being held in jails (awaiting trial or doing time) has also doubled. Finally, the number of juvenile offenders in training schools and private placement has grown substantially. The incapacitation movement has resulted in huge growth in the numbers of blacks and lower-class young adults under correctional supervision and control. More young black males are in penal confinement or under community supervision than are in college. It is estimated that one-fourth of young African American males are under the control of the criminal justice system.

All that having been said, the great revolution in criminal justice in the 20th century has not been in the crime problem but in the criminal justice process. As any student of this process knows, and as many in law enforcement and the prosecutorial and correctional subsystems have yet to accept, court decisions have transformed the face of the process, adding a whole new dimension to it. Never has the term *due process* been more rigorously implemented in all phases of the justice system—from arrest to final release from state control. Such phrases as *Miranda warnings, the exclusionary rule, equity and fairness, arbitrary and capricious decisions, fair trial,* and *inmate rights,* as well as many other concepts and themes, have been forced on the system by federal and higher state courts.

In his book *The Limits of the Criminal Sanction,* Herbert Packer (1968) describes two very different criminal justice models: the due process model in the United States and the crime control, inquisitorial, or social defense model in continental Europe. Packer compares the European crime control model to an assembly line in which the law enforcement arm is the chief element. The police apprehend factually guilty or probably guilty suspects and the other actors in the system—prosecutors, defense attorneys, and judges—play specialized roles in translating probable guilt into legal guilt. As Packer notes of this model, "The image that comes to mind is an assembly line which moves an endless stream of cases, never stopping, carrying them to workers who stand at fixed stations and who perform on each case as it comes by the same small but essential operation that brings it one step closer to being a finished product or . . . a closed file." Further, he notes, "The criminal process is seen as a screening process in which each successive stage . . . involves a series of routinized operations whose success is gauged primarily by their tendency to pass the case along to [successful] conclusion" (p. 21).

In sharp contrast, in the model if not always in practice, the due process model is supposed to operate "as an obstacle course." The general premise is that the movement from probable to legal guilt must be cumbersome and difficult so as to ensure near certainty that persons found guilty are indeed guilty and deserving of punishment. In this approach, there can hardly ever be too many legal hurdles in the process of investigation, arrest, trial, plea, conviction, and disposition. In both models, protection of the public is paramount. In the due process model, an equally important goal is the protection of the rights of suspects as well as those found guilty and those already under state control. The due process model can tolerate some false negatives—guilty persons not arrested, convicted, or sentenced—but it cannot readily tolerate false positives—persons wrongly convicted. The social control model can abide false positives but not false negatives. This puts the two concepts at opposite ends of the philosophical spectrum and leads to irreconcilable conclusions as to the operation of the system, the acted on, and the actors.

This, of course, brings us to the subject of the current volume. Wrongful convictions, however infrequent, are anathema to the American due process system and to all who believe in the fairness of our law enforcement and judicial systems and the constitutional protections guaranteed individual citizens. Not only do such wrongful convictions violate trust in our system, but, as the authors painstakingly assert, such convictions undermine public safety by leaving the "true" positives—the guilty—in the community to commit future grave offenses.

As I know from personal contact with all the authors, this book has been a decade or more in the making. The volume expresses their deeply held commitment to due process and the need to protect equally society, the families and loved ones of crime victims, and the false positives from the inevitable errors that all human institutions sometimes make—unintentionally, accidentally, or through failures in the workings of the system known popularly as snafus (and by many less delicate names as well). In a moderate voice, this book examines the painful issues in wrongful conviction. The focus is geared to answering the core questions: How often does it happen? Why does it happen? How does it happen? To whom does it happen? How can it be prevented from happening? How should the wrongfully convicted be made whole again—what constitutes adequate compensation?

In this well-researched and fascinating volume, Huff, Rattner, and Sagarin mix materials from case files in the literature and those reported in numerous research reports and in the media. They present a great deal of information on research studies, both national and international, concerning the accuracy of eyewitness perceptions. Interviews with individuals who have been wrongly convicted and subsequently exonerated, as well as with some of the actors in the system are included, as are trial documents, court transcripts, and media reports on trials. There is no other book available on the "guilty" but innocent with such a broad focus and so much rich detail. It is a good read, indeed.

The authors begin by discussing some celebrated cases—some known to the general reader, but most known only to specialists. These celebrated historic cases include the Salem witchcraft cases; the Alfred Dreyfus accusation, trial, punishment, and exoneration; the recent release after conviction and imprisonment of "Ivan the Terrible" Demjanjuk, and the famous miscarriage of justice in the case of the "Scottsboro Boys." (As an aside, when I was so young that I could not quite understand the meaning of the Scottsboro boys' trial and conviction, I remember the street demonstrations and torchlight parades in my community and the marchers shouting, "The Scottsboro boys shall not die!" Fortunately, they did not die, even though eight of the nine black youths were initially sentenced to death for the rapes of two white girls—rapes that never occurred and that were later recanted.) Some readers may also remember the Leo Frank conviction and his lynching by a mob while in custody. More recently, there have been the sagas of Randall Adams and the Jacksons. But hardly anyone is likely to know much about Isidore Zimmerman, his 24 years in prison, the commutation of his sentence 2 hours before execution, his 20 subsequent years spent seeking compensation after his prison release, and his death shortly after receiving $1 million for wrongful imprisonment.

One of the major contributions of this volume is the attempt to get at some sort of reliable estimate of the incidence of wrongful conviction in the United States per annum. Based on a questionnaire submitted to experienced criminal justice actors in Ohio—police administrators, sheriffs, county prosecutors, public defenders, and criminal court bench judges—0.5% of those convicted of felonies are estimated to be innocent of the crimes charged. The authors are quick to point out that these more than 10,000 convicted innocents (index crimes alone) were not necessarily without previous criminal involvement. Indeed, for some, their prior records may have led to their arrest and conviction.

Assuming the accuracy, or even near reliability, of the above estimate, there are many prisoners who have served or are serving time who might well be the subjects of a subsequent book on the innocent but "guilty." The question, then, is why innocents, whatever their actual number, are found guilty. Why does our cherished due process obstacle course flatten into a straightaway? What happens to all the hurdles?

The authors contend that although becoming legally guilty though factually innocent is the result of interaction among several factors, faulty eyewitness identification is the most critical of these variables and alone accounts for as many as half of all erroneous findings of legal guilt. Experiments have shown that race and ethnicity are also crucial in eyewitness mistakes; so are physical conditions such as lighting, angle of sight, and length of observation. These errors, in themselves, are usually insufficient in the face of diligent investigation; however, when coupled with overzealousness, biases, and ineptitude on the part of some police officers, lawyers, and prosecutors, and pressure for convictions from the community and elected officials, erroneous eyewitness identifications are more than enough to convict.

Furthermore, in our criminal justice system, where the same actors may participate in many arrests, prosecutions, and trials over a number of years, there tend to develop interactional bonds that are hard to overcome. Thus, as the erroneous conviction case makes its way up the line, there is considerable reluctance to override the "evidence" and judgments made at the preceding levels. Instead of a hurdle, there is instead the "ratification of error." This is no different from the working codes and internal cultures in other endeavors—medicine (as in malpractice), law, industry. Loyalty tends to override doubt and even experience. Cases are inexorably pushed forward.

The authors also include a chapter on the dynamics of obtaining and using doubtful (false) confessions. Faced with the possibility of going to trial for murder, and the uncertainty of the outcome, some defendants conclude (as may their public defenders or even their personal lawyers) that plea-bargained prison stretches are the safer option. There is also the possibility that a suspect's refusal to accept a plea bargain will influence the severity of his or her sentence—if convicted.

In the last chapter, the authors suggest public and professional consideration of 14 policy recommendations growing out of this decade of research. I will mention only the last one here, which pertains to irreversible errors. Huff, Rattner, and Sagarin suggest the substitution of life sentences, without the possibility of parole, in all death penalty cases. Some of their other recommendations are no less interesting and controversial. All are worth your consideration and the consideration of lawmakers on the judiciary committees in legislatures around the country.

—Simon Dinitz
Professor Emeritus
Ohio State University

Acknowledgments

We have received a great deal of valuable assistance and encouragement throughout the course of our research and during the preparation of this manuscript.[1] As for the initial idea to conduct a study of wrongful convictions—both the cases and the processes—we are indebted to our friend and colleague the late Professor Edward Sagarin, whom we have also acknowledged in our dedication. Ed contributed more than ideas; he wrote some of the initial material for this book (which we have incorporated almost entirely verbatim), and his enthusiasm and encouragement were always there for us. Since his death, his widow, Gert, has maintained a genuine interest in this book, one of Ed's last writing projects.

We are also indebted to the many judges, prosecutors, defense attorneys, and law enforcement officers who have been willing to complete our surveys, and who also (in many cases) have informally shared their experiences and their insights with us over the past decade, both in the

United States and in Israel. This book documents the fact that wrongful convictions often result, at least in part, from incompetent, unprofessional, and/or unethical conduct by law enforcement officers, prosecutors, defense attorneys, and even judges. However, we firmly believe that the great majority of those working in the criminal justice system are genuinely concerned about such errors and their implications for justice and for public safety.

For their assistance and collaboration in analyzing cases of wrongful conviction and compensation in the state of Ohio, we would like to thank Professor Anand Desai of the School of Public Policy and Management at Ohio State; Howard Ishiyama, a doctoral candidate at that institution; and Jack Jones and Ted Stanich, former graduate research associates. Our appreciation also goes to Martin Yant, a courageous journalist and author who has published many newspaper articles and a book on wrongful conviction, for his assistance in updating and summarizing some of the cases discussed in this book. Marty exemplifies the kind of independent inquiry and dedication to the pursuit of truth that is essential to a free, democratic society.

Two distinguished scholars—professors Rita Simon of the American University and Elizabeth Loftus of the University of Washington—reviewed portions of the manuscript prior to its publication and made many useful and insightful suggestions for improvement, which we have attempted to incorporate. We want to recognize their important contributions while at the same time acknowledging that we are solely responsible for the content of the book and the degree to which it meets, or fails to meet, its purpose: describing and analyzing the problem of wrongful conviction and its public policy implications.

Ms. Georgia Meyer, administrative secretary at Ohio State's Criminal Justice Research Center, helped immensely in coordinating the production of the final manuscript. She also remained characteristically cheerful in spite of deadline pressures.

We owe a special debt of gratitude to some of the convicted innocents and their families for sharing their experiences—injustice, trauma, and, ultimately, vindication. Special recognition goes to Randall Dale Adams, Bradley Cox, Lenell Geter, Todd Neely, and Todd's parents, Edith and Lewis Crosley, for their openness and their willingness to let us try to learn what the experience of wrongful conviction means on a personal and familial level. The insights they provided helped shape much of what is in this book, which is, after all, their story.

Finally, we express our love and appreciation to our own families for their patience with us over the past decade as we pursued our analysis of this important problem. We can never compensate them for the time we stole; we can only hope that this book will make a small contribution to the continuing pursuit of social and criminal justice throughout the world.

C. RONALD HUFF
ARYE RATTNER

Note

1. We have contributed equally to the research and writing of this book, and our names are therefore displayed alphabetically.

Introduction

The concept of justice is timeless, as is the corresponding concern about convicting an innocent person. Indeed, as Daniel Webster once proclaimed, "Justice, sir, is the greatest interest of man on earth."

This book addresses a specific kind of injustice—wrongful conviction. The topic, in addition to being timeless, is also timely. As we write this, the case of John Demjanjuk, accused of being "Ivan the Terrible," a Nazi death camp guard who helped in the mass murder of Jews, is being played out on the world's stage. Sharing that international stage within the recent past have been two cases on different continents. First is the wrongful conviction and imprisonment (for 16 years) of the "Birmingham Six," alleged members of the Irish Republican Army, for the bombing of two British pubs. This case (which inspired the film *In the Name of the Father*) led to a high-level review of the entire British criminal justice system, which regularly receives scrutiny through a popular television series titled *Rough Justice*. Second is the tragic wrongful conviction of Lindy and

Michael Chamberlain, an Australian couple whose trial and wrongful conviction in the death of their infant daughter inspired the movie *A Cry in the Dark*. The Chamberlains were awarded $320,000 in compensation by the Australian government.

The wrongful conviction theme is also important in American popular culture, as reflected in the runaway hit movie attraction *The Fugitive*. In the movie, Harrison Ford plays the role of Dr. Richard Kimble, a physician who is wrongfully convicted of murdering his wife and who claims that a one-armed intruder was the actual murderer. The movie, and the popular former television series of the same name, is loosely based on the actual wrongful conviction of Dr. Sam Sheppard, an Ohio physician imprisoned for life in 1954 for the murder of his wife.

In the pages that follow, we shall attempt to define, describe, and analyze the problem of wrongful conviction and its implications for society. Not everyone will be pleased with our definition, because we do not include a number of cases in which it is clear that injustice occurred. By our restrictive definition of wrongful conviction, even the case of Jesus would not qualify, because Jesus' behavior, in the name of righteousness, did violate the laws of his day, unfair as they were. We focus here on cases in which the convicted persons did not commit the crimes alleged—in other words, they are behaviorally innocent of the crimes.

We present for the reader's consideration survey data concerning the possible magnitude of the problem and its causes; actual cases of wrongful conviction, as well as some in which doubt remains; detailed analyses of each of the major factors associated with wrongful conviction and how these factors interact; and, finally, a discussion of the public policy implications of our research, including some recommendations for reducing the occurrence of this problem, identifying and compensating those who are wrongfully convicted, and eliminating (or greatly curtailing) the possibility of executing innocent persons.

We will demonstrate that the American system of criminal justice is so large and has so many arrests each year that even if the system were 99.5% accurate, it would still generate more than 10,000 wrongful convictions a year for the eight serious index crimes alone (these eight crimes are murder and nonnegligent manslaughter, forcible rape, aggravated assault, robbery, burglary, larceny-theft, motor vehicle theft, and arson). It is likely that the error rate is even higher for less serious crimes, making it highly probable that wrongful conviction affects a great many Americans each year, even though the error rate may be relatively small.

Finally, throughout the volume we shall attempt to dispel a common, but fallacious, assumption about this topic: that wrongful conviction is an issue that should inherently interest "liberals" more than "conservatives" (who are presumed to be more interested in "law and order" and "public safety"). We attempt to refute this assumption by noting (and vividly illustrating, in many of our cases) that every time an innocent offender is wrongfully convicted, the actual offender typically remains free to continue victimizing the public. Thus, this book concerns a problem that affects not only an individual's right to due process and a fair trial, but also a serious public safety concern. The reader will learn about murders, rapes, and other serious crimes that were permitted to occur because the wrong person was arrested for a given crime.

Finally, we present a framework for understanding this problem within the overall context of the American criminal justice system. Drawing on Packer's (1968) contrasting "crime control" and "due process" models, we illustrate how this conceptual framework can be useful for increasing our understanding of the problem of wrongful conviction and for the formulation of public policy recommendations to reduce the frequency with which it occurs. Although no system of justice can be perfect, we believe that if efforts are focused on *preventable* errors, the U.S. system can substantially reduce the kinds of injustices discussed in the pages that follow. It would be well worth the effort, and it is our hope that this volume may contribute to that end.

1

With Apologies to the Prisoner

It is better to risk saving a guilty person than to condemn an innocent one.
Voltaire, *Zadig,* 1747

It is better that ten guilty persons escape than one innocent suffer.
Sir William Blackstone, *Commentaries,* 1765-1769

During the 1980s and early 1990s, the American conscience was shaken by a number of instances that cast doubt on a cherished belief—that innocent people are seldom, if ever, convicted and imprisoned, and they are certainly not executed. Almost as if orchestrated in the way they came to public attention, completely unrelated cases of miscarriage of justice, not in which the guilty were freed but in which the totally innocent were severely punished, became front-page news and the subject of frequent discussion on television. Nor were the charges trivial: Most of the convictions were for murder or rape.

In the state of Ohio, Bradley Cox, a white youth found guilty of rape on the basis of a repudiated confession given to the police after a *Miranda* warning had been issued, had served 2 years of a 56- to 200-year term when the actual rapist, Jon Simonis (the "ski-mask rapist"), confessed and Cox was released from prison. There is irony in the fact that in the same state, at about the same time, a black man who had served 5 years in prison for a series of rapes he had not committed was likewise released when the true rapist was found. It added a further dimension of public wonder that the innocent and the guilty man had the same last name, and they came to be known as "the right Jackson" and "the wrong Jackson" ("Freed Jackson's Advice," 1982).

These cases were very much in the news when Isidore Zimmerman died. This man had once been on death row in New York; his head had been shaven in readiness for the electrodes 2 hours before his sentence was commuted to life imprisonment and before the switch would send lethal electricity through his body. Protesting his innocence, he served 24 years before he was released, completely exonerated, then spent another 20 years struggling to gain some compensation for his wrongful imprisonment. Finally, he won his case; an elderly and broken man, he was awarded $1 million for the wrongs done to him by the state of New York, and he died 4 months later ("Isidore Zimmerman," 1983).

Zimmerman's case was still unforgotten when Ludovic Kennedy, a prominent British investigative journalist, published his book *The Airman and the Carpenter* (1985a), which left little doubt in the minds of most readers that Bruno Richard Hauptmann had been innocent of the kidnapping and murder of the Lindbergh baby some 50 years earlier. Back in New York, Nathaniel Carter, a religious man with an impeccable record, was freed from prison after having been convicted of the murder of his estranged wife's foster mother, for which he had been given a life sentence, when it was discovered that the chief witness against him (his former wife) had committed the murder and had now confessed to it, under immunity ("How Errors Convicted," 1984).

At about the same time full pages in the newspapers were being devoted to Carter, along came a case that caught the public's imagination and that remained in the headlines for a long period: the controversial case of Gary Dotson and his former accuser, Cathleen Crowell, now married and known as Cathleen Webb. In 1979, Gary Dotson, who was 22 years old, white, and had previously been in minor trouble with the police for nonviolent crimes, was found guilty of raping Cathleen Crowell. Protesting his innocence, he was sentenced to 25 to 50 years in prison. Against him was the victim's description to the police of the rapist (a description she was to claim, 6 years later, was entirely fictional); then, when she was shown photographs of possible suspects by the police, she picked one that at least superficially resembled the description she had given—a young man with long blond hair and a mustache. There was no medical testimony that associated the defendant with the rape; there was only his denial, and some confusing alibis. For 6 years Dotson remained in prison, insisting on his innocence; so far as is known, there was no contact between him and the woman who had accused him. Then Cathleen Webb resurfaced and made a complete recantation; she stated that she had never been raped, that in 1979 she had had sexual relations with a boyfriend and feared repercussions from her foster parents if she were pregnant. Now she was coming forward out of pangs of conscience and because she had found religion (Webb & Chapian, 1985).

Gary Dotson was freed on bond, but the original judge who had heard the case 6 years earlier did not believe the recantation, and sent him back to prison. There was a public outcry, and in 1987 the governor of Illinois made a Solomonic decision in an effort to please everyone: He would not grant a pardon but would commute the sentence to time already served (longer than the average served for rape) because Dotson had suffered enough. At the same time, he asserted his belief that Dotson was guilty and that the victim's original testimony was true and her recantation false. At any rate, Dotson was "free" to walk away, but he was burdened by his ordeal, his notoriety, and a felony conviction. After a jail term for parole violation, he was finally cleared of the rape charge in 1989, when DNA testing ruled him out as the rapist (Yant, 1991).

It is especially interesting that Dotson's case caused so much furor over the conviction of the innocent, because it was the one case among the many that came to light at the time in which innocence was not well established. A cloud of doubt hung over the Dotson case until improved DNA testing provided the crucial exculpatory evidence. But if it took a case with some lingering doubts to make the conviction of the innocent an issue of national attention, there were many others in which no such doubt existed. One need only consider the trilogy of injustices done in Dallas to Lenell Geter, Randall Dale Adams, and Joyce Ann Brown and these individuals' wrongful convictions to appreciate that the presumption

of innocence is at best fragile and at worst a romantic fantasy once a
suitable suspect has been arrested, charged, and placed at risk in our most
imperfect "adversarial" system of justice. (We discuss the "Dallas trilogy"
in detail in Chapter 2.)

The distinguished jurist Learned Hand stated in 1923, "Our procedure
has always been haunted by the ghost of the innocent man convicted. It
is an unreal dream" (*United States v. Garsson,* 1923). Innocent people,
Justice Hand contended, were not in our prisons. He did not qualify his
statement, or even suggest that there may be a few instances, or even a
single instance now and then, or that these things once happened frequently in the South as a result of racial prejudice but no longer occurred
(a statement that he could hardly have made in 1923). It is an astounding
statement, belied by the actual events before and during Justice Hand's
days on the bench, and subsequently, too. He could not have been ignorant
of the former and should have been able to foresee the latter.[1]

The best that can be said of Hand's remark is that it was meant
figuratively; he wished to contest the notion that the prisons were filled
with innocents. If that is all he was saying, we do not dispute it. The
prisons are not *filled* with innocents—but next month or the one after will
witness at least one more case of a prisoner coming before a judge who
will tell him or her, "New evidence has been uncovered that demonstrates
that you are innocent, and we send you forth, a free man [or woman] in a
free America." And the judge might add: "Sorry for the inconvenience."

The old cliché that it is better for 10 guilty men to go free than for a
single innocent person to be found guilty and imprisoned is a viewpoint
held by few, although paid lip service by many. It is a statement breached
so often in practice that its repetition is cynical. Furthermore, it is our
contention, as we will show throughout this work, that there is an impli-
cation that is fundamentally untrue in such a maxim, because finding one
innocent person guilty is not only an unnecessary price for us to pay in
human waste and tragedy for the preservation of our criminal justice
system, but it often results in the closing of cases with actual perpetrators
still at large to continue to commit crimes. Furthermore, the conviction of
the innocent serves to cast doubt upon the reliability of the criminal justice
system and hence may assist in exculpating the genuinely guilty.

Most of the cases of wrongful conviction that come to public attention
involve murder or rape, if only because of the severity of the sentences
for such offenses and, in the case of murder, implications for the death

penalty. We describe one particular case of rape below, one we shall mention in the pages to come because of the lessons that it illustrates.

A woman in Dubuque, Iowa, is raped by a stranger—there is no dispute about this fact in the case—and after the event she runs out into a crowded street, screaming with understandable hysteria, and identifies a man in the crowd as having just committed the heinous act. David Feddersen is arrested, but statistically at least, he has a few things going for him: He is white (but so was the rapist); he was walking along a street that he regularly took at that time of day, and he has never been involved in a violent crime, or in violence as such. He was not hurrying or running when seized, although he had been a member of his high school track team, and could easily have escaped had he wished.

Against him was the eyewitness identification, community pressure to catch rapists, and the fact that, in the words of his mother, "he had been in trouble with the law before." Of course, he had no alibi—he was indeed among the crowd when the woman came running after the attacker. But so were many other people. On the other hand, that she could identify him so certainly and with no hesitation so soon after the event seemed to indicate some possibility of guilt. The fact that she had no corroborating witnesses was to be expected: People do not generally go around committing rape in the presence of others, unless it is a group rape, with two or more rapists collaborating against one victim.

At the time he was seized and identified by the victim, David Feddersen was walking at a normal pace, not as if he were trying to lose himself among many or attempting to get away. His demeanor, then, was not particularly damaging. With no medical testimony, it came down to the victim's word against that of the accused; she was certain that he was guilty, and he was even more certain that he was innocent. By unanimous vote of an Iowa jury that his lawyer had helped to choose, Feddersen was declared guilty of rape.

He was stunned. Knowing he was innocent, he was positive that he would be exonerated. When he rose to speak in court, he was not contrite but arrogant. Asked if he had anything to say before sentence was pronounced, he showed anger, denounced the court, the jury, and the complaining witness, and demonstrated neither sympathy for the victim nor remorse for what he had done—which would have been difficult, considering he had not done anything. Perhaps in part as a result of his own behavior, and in part because the judge had only limited leeway in deciding on the punishment to be meted out to the man who was now a convicted felon, Feddersen received a lengthy prison term. By happenstance, coincidence, and dogged effort on his own part, and aided by his family's belief in him, after 2 years in prison Feddersen was able to convince all parties in the case except the complaining victim to admit their error. Police, prosecutors, and judge were certain, because of new evidence that had been uncovered, that they had sent the wrong man to prison.

Taken back to court, standing before the same judge who had once sentenced him, he was told that a mistake had been made, that his innocence was clearly established, and that he should now turn around and walk out through the front door of the court, a free man. The judge said that the fact that an innocent man could be found guilty "is scary." A reporter asked a prosecutor what had gone wrong with this case, and the prosecutor answered, "No man is entitled to a perfect trial. He is entitled to a fair trail, but the verdict was wrong. Mr. Feddersen received a fair trial." This is a most cynical and inadequate answer. It is true that no one is entitled to a perfect trial, because perfection is always unattainable. It may be true that he received a fair trial—he had adequate counsel, no confession had been obtained, no exculpating evidence had been suppressed, no damaging evidence had been manufactured. But the prosecutor omitted any reference to what the reporter was seeking, and what we are all entitled to know, namely, what goes wrong with a criminal justice system that produces a case like Feddersen's, and many others. The judge said that it was scary that such a thing could happen. We find it equally frightening that, after such a thing takes place, it is often cavalierly dismissed, with no effort made to understand how it might have been averted.

Another case that is relevant here involves the question of reasonable doubt. In this volume we devote only little attention to persons formerly or currently in prison whose innocence has not been established but about whom there is considerable and reasonable doubt as to guilt. This is not our major focus, but the following case is so replete with ironies and contradictions that it is worthy of study. James Hicks, 31 years of age, had served 7 years of a 10-year sentence in the state of Maine for the murder of his wife. On the witness stand he had denied that he killed her, but readily admitted that he had been living with another woman for about 5 years prior to the disappearance of his wife, and that he had two children with this woman, to whom he was not married. One of the unusual aspects of the case, but by no means unique in murder trials, was that the body of the wife had never been found. The presence of a dead body is not an absolute must for a murder conviction—after all, a murderer can throw a victim overboard somewhere on the ocean, and the body might never be found—guilt can be established beyond a reasonable doubt by witnesses' testimony, evidence of motive, and other evidence. In this case, there were no witnesses. The wife disappeared and was not heard of again. Hicks believes that his wife walked away and never came back—and that she may well know that he is in prison for her murder.

After 7 years in prison, Hicks applied for permission to marry the mother of his two children, with whom he had maintained a romance through all his difficulties. In Maine and in many other states, a prisoner and a free person may marry if permission is granted by the authorities. But here an unexpected irony enters the case. Hicks was denied a license to get married on the grounds that if the state allowed the marriage it might be an accomplice in the act of bigamy. No marriage license could be issued without a death certificate for Hicks's apparently dead wife or a divorce decree. The Medical Services Office refused to issue a death certificate because there was no body, and Hicks refused to sign a statement acknowledging that he knew his wife was dead—which would have cleared the way for the death certificate and the marriage, but would have been, in effect, a confession of guilt. This he would not make, because the suggestion of murder would violate his contention that his wife had just walked away. So, although he was convicted of murdering his wife on the basis of evidence that convinced 12 men and women beyond a reasonable doubt, the authorities entertained some doubt that his wife was dead.

If we place this convict in the group of currently confined people about whose guilt there is slight doubt but not in the group whose innocence is definitely established, then the authorities must convince us that we are wrong. At least some people have not slight but reasonable doubt, among them the prison authorities and others with access to records. And if the doubt is reasonable enough to prevent a marriage, then the guilty verdict cannot meet the standard of guilt beyond a reasonable doubt. One is tempted to speak of this prisoner as living in a Kafkaesque world, but perhaps his case is just another sad example of what we have come to call, in homage to Joseph Heller, a catch-22 situation.

The fact that innocent people are occasionally convicted and later exonerated has long been one of the major arguments against capital punishment. In this century the United States and England have seen several cases of executed people whose innocence was later established and could not be disputed; many executed even when there was great doubt as to their guilt; and numerous others, all innocent, whose lives were saved from the hands of the executioner only after appeals, the granting of clemency, commutations, or the collapse of what had appeared to be airtight cases. Two major instances of executions of the innocent have been described in detail by Ludovic Kennedy. In *Ten Rillington Place,* Kennedy (1961/1985b) tells the story of the arrest, trial, and hanging of Timothy Evans. The crime for which Evans gave his life was actually committed by the chief witness against him, a man named Christie, who was later caught and hanged. The case and Kennedy's book about it are often cited as responsible for the abolition of capital punishment in England. More recently, Kennedy (1985a) has presented an extraordinarily strong argument that Bruno Hauptmann did not kill the Lindbergh baby. It is also generally believed that Sacco and Vanzetti were not guilty, although this is not a unanimous view.

Indeed, Bedau and Radelet (1987), after conducting an exhaustive study of wrongful conviction in capital, or potentially capital, cases, reached the conclusion that 23 innocent persons were executed in the United States between 1905 and 1974, and 22 others had "close calls" (reprieves came within 72 hours of their scheduled executions). It should be noted that Bedau and Radelet's classification of these cases as errors is not universally accepted, and their study has received both praise and criticism (see, for example, Markman & Cassell, 1988).

Of several thousand legal and extralegal executions of blacks in the South between 1875 and 1955, and a few lynchings of whites both in and outside the South, we consider here only the legal executions, and the evidence that many of those executed were innocent persons, particularly when the charge was rape, is overwhelming. But the legal apparatus cannot be exonerated when it arrests a man and finds him guilty, fails to protect him, and allows citizens to carry out his execution, a not uncommon practice at one time, as described by William Faulkner in his short story "Dry September."

Many have been sentenced to die and had their sentences commuted, served long prison terms, and then were exonerated. All but one of the

"Scottsboro boys" were sentenced to death, and only worldwide protest that focused attention on this injustice saved their lives. No one today disputes that these young men were innocent; in fact, the sole survivor of the nine was welcomed by the governor of Alabama when he returned there in the early 1980s.

Most important, it seems to us, is that there is often considerable doubt as to guilt. In *Against the Evidence* (1970), Logan tells the story of the only police officer ever to be executed by the state of New York. Logan contends that Lieutenant Becker was innocent, and amasses considerable detail to establish her point. A reader of her work and a follower of the story of this notorious and controversial case may not be as convinced of Becker's innocence as Logan is, but one cannot close Logan's book without a strong doubt as to Becker's guilt.

Like Timothy Evans in England (Kennedy, 1961/1985b), Nathaniel Carter in New York State was found guilty of murder almost solely on the basis of the testimony of the actual killer. Sentenced to life imprisonment, he served 2 years, at which time the witness (Evans's former wife) came forward and, under complete immunity, testified that she had committed the crime. This case has been cited as an example of the classic argument against the death penalty. In response to this use of the case as an example, one judge who is among the proponents of capital punishment said in a letter to the *New York Times* that Carter could not (or would not) have received execution as punishment, even if it had been legal at the time in the state of New York, because he had no previous criminal record. This assertion is incorrect, however, on both legal and factual grounds. In states that have capital punishment, the distinction between persons with and without previous criminal records is not made, and when New York State had the death penalty on its books there was no such distinction. In fact, some of the most notorious executions in New York State were carried out on people who did not have flawed records: Lieutenant Becker, Ruth Snyder, and Judd Gray, among others. Those convicted of murder are eligible for execution, if they meet all other legal requirements and state law permits it, regardless of the purity of their previous records. In fact, at any given time there are on death row persons with no record even of previous *arrests*. Many first-time offenders, innocent and guilty, have gone to their deaths at the hands of the executioner, and Carter could well have been among them, the above-mentioned judge's comment notwithstanding.

It is sometimes argued by those who favor capital punishment that if only those whose guilt is distinctly and indubitably apparent are executed, this will eliminate the chances of any posthumous exonerations. This is belied by history, however, including recent history: The factors that lead to the sentence of death rather than a long prison term include such variables as the heinousness of the crime attributed to the accused and the ages and races of both perpetrator and victim; certainly not taken into account is whether or not guilt has been firmly established. The concept in American and English law is that, whether for a minor or a major crime, and regardless of the punishment, proof of guilt must be established beyond a reasonable doubt. There is no provision for—nor do we know of any responsible jurist, philosopher of law, or criminologist who would advocate—a finding of guilt when there is reasonable doubt, with a lesser punishment just in case a mistake is being made.

Defining the Convicted Innocents

We have carved out for study in this work a group that is not easy to define and that excludes many who are wrongfully incarcerated. This is not a book about injustice broadly defined, but about one special aspect of injustice, the conviction of an innocent person.

Convicted innocents, as defined here, are people who have been arrested on criminal charges, although not necessarily armed robbery, rape, or murder; who have either pleaded guilty to the charge or have been tried and found guilty; and who, notwithstanding plea or verdict, are in fact innocent. Although we shall present estimates of the extent of this phenomenon among felony cases, our discussions and conclusions will revolve around those who have been clearly exculpated, either because the alleged crime was never committed or, more frequently, the convicted person was not the perpetrator. Many convicted innocents have committed other crimes, but are nonetheless innocent of the specific charges of which they have been accused and convicted.

This definition excludes from our discussion several important groups. From the viewpoint of injustice, the most significant of these groups consists of people who have been held before trial for considerable periods of time, many months or even years, and then exonerated, with their innocence either admitted by the prosecution and the police or so clearly established as to be beyond question. Matzner and English (1973) have written about a case in which four people were held in a New Jersey jail on murder charges for which the evidence was utterly absurd, but because the charge was first-degree murder, punishable by death, no bail was allowed. Two of the individuals held were a couple, middle-class publishers of a local community newspaper; the third was one of their employees, and the fourth was a fairly high-ranking police officer who was arrested and charged with the murder when he objected to the manner in which the investigation was being handled. The case involved false arrest, prosecutorial and police improprieties, and incarceration without crime. But despite the suffering imposed on these four people and their families, their case does not fall within the purview of our study, because our major interest is in the factors that contribute to the malfunctioning of a legal system that results in false *conviction* (including the false plea of guilty).

Our definition excludes those found not guilty in a second trial, or on appeal, because of the exclusion of crucial evidence stemming from illegal searches and seizures or other violations of suspects' rights. To be sure, such people were once convicted and today stand legally not guilty, but there is a significant difference between being found "not guilty" according to the standards of our legal system and establishing complete innocence. In many of these cases complete exoneration cannot be inferred from subsequent acquittals or reversals. So it is with the case of Claus von Bulow, which provides an excellent example of the difference between having a conviction reversed on appeal and the establishment of innocence. Convicted on two counts of attempting to murder his wealthy and socially prominent wife, Martha (Sunny) von Bulow, of Newport, Rhode Island, von Bulow had his conviction overturned in 1984 by the Rhode Island Supreme Court, which ruled that there had been an illegal search that resulted in toxicological testing and that the subsequent expert testimony by the state's toxicologist was therefore inadmissible. In making this ruling, the Rhode Island Supreme Court argued that the language of the Rhode Island Constitution permitted the application of a more exacting standard than that required by the U.S. Constitution as interpreted by the U.S. Supreme Court.

Miranda and Escobedo both had their guilty verdicts overturned, but neither of them qualifies for inclusion in this study of convicted innocents, any more than would someone who was found not guilty by reason of insanity at a second trial. These are people whose factual guilt, rather than legally established guilt, has not been effectively disputed. But this is not the place to discuss the rationale of a criminal justice system that will free a person generally or almost universally believed to be guilty of a major crime because of procedural defects rather than substantive error. In such instances, it is not the innocence of the accused that has been established, but the unfairness governing his or her arrest and conviction. It is that unfairness the courts seek to deter by overturning convictions reached through violations of the rights of the accused.

Like many others, we are concerned with the many guilty persons who "beat the rap" because of good lawyers or fine technicalities or intimidation of witnesses, who then fear to testify against them. These persons far outnumber the convicted innocents, of that we are certain. They are examples of justice gone wrong, sometimes for defensible reasons (as when a true confession is excluded because it was obtained by illegal trickery or force), but more often for reasons that dismay those who recognize the enormity of the crime problem, especially in the United States. In fact, when we first began our research on wrongful conviction, we surveyed judges and other public officials and received this reply from one Ohio judge: "I am deeply disappointed that my old university is even remotely involved in this type of venture. Aren't there more pressing topics in this world that your efforts can be funneled to?" (Huff, Rattner, & Sagarin, 1986, p. 522).

Why, then, concentrate on what is probably the small percentage of convicted innocents and ignore the far more numerous and, in some respects, more threatening problem of the opposite, the judicially released guilty? There are many answers to this question. Both sides of the coin deserve attention, but the one we focus on has received it only in unrelated stories that have hit the newspapers. Both problems deserve study to determine what can be done to reduce injustice and undeserved pain and suffering; here we focus on one, and others will concentrate elsewhere. Finally, as we will argue in our concluding chapter, we believe that the two problems are interrelated in two important ways: (a) The conviction of the innocent leaves the guilty free to commit more crimes, thus threatening public safety; and (b) each instance of the conviction of an innocent enhances the possibility that there will be more not-guilty verdicts against the truly guilty.

Where Doubt Remains

Although from time to time in this volume we will mention some cases of people currently in prison, we shall not place our major attention on them. Nor can we, of course, discuss those cases that will surface next month or next year. Every study of people in prison shows a rather sizable minority who proclaim their innocence, but examination of the court records usually convinces researchers that most of those making this claim are not at all innocent. We believe, however, that there are quite a few men and women in prison, and some on death row, who, higher courts' rulings to the contrary, have been convicted in ways that leave considerable doubt as to their guilt or, to use the technical expression, were not convicted by evidence that established guilt beyond a reasonable doubt. There are also borderline cases. In our view, prisoners who do not meet the legal standards of guilt should be free, but we cannot be certain that they were or are convicted innocents, and we therefore exclude them from our study.

One such man was Bill Phillips, a "bad cop" who was always on the take. Trapped by his own venality, involved not only in bribery but in intimate relationships with pimps and prostitutes, he was finally left with no choice but to testify openly about police corruption, including his own, before the Knapp Commission, which investigated such misconduct in New York City. He testified under immunity from prosecution for bribery, extortion, and other crimes in which he had participated and that he described in detail, although his testimony would not protect him from departmental action that could be taken against him and that would affect his pension and other retirement benefits.

Many members of the New York Police Department were no doubt embarrassed by the testimony of Phillips. Watching the bad cop testifying on television, a rather high-ranking police officer suddenly recognized Phillips himself as a man who was wanted for murder. He passed the word to other members of his squad, and soon there was an entire group ready to testify as to Phillips's guilt. As the murder of which Phillips was accused had taken place considerably earlier, the defense had some difficulty establishing an alibi: It was hard to say exactly where Phillips had been that night. That he knew the woman who had been murdered, and that she was a prostitute in the group with which he mingled, was never denied.

As bad a cop as Phillips was, he was even worse as a suspect and then as a defendant. Rather than say that he did not know where he had been on the night of the murder, he fabricated some testimony that he had not thought out very carefully and that was easily refuted. But the prosecution rejected the inclusion of the major point the defense wanted to establish and the judge excluded it from testimony, a ruling held to be legal by the highest court at which the case could be appealed. The defense's point was that the "recognition" and the "discovery" were far-fetched ruses deliberately concocted by high-ranking police as a warning to any other officer who might think of testifying with regard to police corruption. The judge and the higher courts ruled that the motive of the prosecution witnesses was not at issue, but only their credibility. Phillips was convicted and his appeals were denied; to this day, it is difficult for a reasonable person to refute the possibility that he may be a convicted innocent.

In Chapter 5, we present the story of George Whitmore: how he confessed to crimes that he had not committed, the tremendous publicity around his confession, the publicity when it started to fall apart, and how his was the only confession cited by the U.S. Supreme Court in the statement by the majority of the court explaining why the *Miranda* warnings are needed (Lefkowitz & Gross, 1969). The case left the New York Police Department in considerable embarrassment, not only because of the exposure of a false confession, but because the murders to which Whitmore had confessed were the most sensational, notorious, and headline grabbing of the year, if not the decade. There was increased pressure to solve the crime, and a known criminal, Michael Delaney, went to the police and gave them the name of the killer in exchange for complete immunity, not merely on drug deals and robberies *but on a murder charge* as well. Delaney and the police made their deal, and then Delaney told them the name of a friend who had come to his home some months before and announced, "I just iced two broads." Rickie Robles was arrested, and after a complex case fought over questions of admissibility of evidence and alleged violation of the *Miranda* rules by the police, was found guilty. Robles maintained his innocence, a contention accepted by some who have studied the case in detail (Lefkowitz & Gross, 1969). In our study he stands with Phillips and many others: The evidence for his guilt or innocence is not clear-cut, and he remains in a doubtful category. But the present work is not focused on those like Phillips and Robles; rather, it is confined to cases where conviction took place and there was an indisputable error.

Still another New York case illustrates the uncertainty surrounding the guilt of some of those who are convicted. A white student in Brooklyn, studying art at Pratt Institute, was robbed. Two weeks after the robbery, he saw a black man standing on a street corner, pointed him out to police as the man who had committed the robbery, and Michael MacCray was arrested. MacCray had no previous record. Certainly the evidence against him was hardly overwhelming; it did not merely fail to meet the standard of guilt beyond a reasonable doubt, it did not even come close. The case was tried before a jury of nine whites and three blacks, and it was a hung jury, said to have been clearly divided by race. MacCray was retried, and this time the district attorney, Eugene Gold, made sure that the jury was all white by using his peremptory challenges (generally, challenges to prospective jurors that can be made without giving any reason whatsoever) against seven blacks and one Hispanic. The remaining jurors, all white, brought in a verdict of guilty.

The MacCray case was appealed with the assistance of the New York Civil Liberties Union, which argued that, precedent notwithstanding, peremptory challenges cannot be used to obtain a jury of a desired racial or ethnic composition. By the time of the appeal Gold was no longer district attorney, but his successor, Elizabeth Holtzman, true to the canons of the adversary system, opposed the appeal, denying that her predecessor had used race and at the same time upholding his right to use peremptory challenges in any manner he wished (the number of peremptory challenges is severely limited for both sides, and thus there would be some restraint on their abuse or misuse). Although the decision in the case went against the office of the district attorney, Holtzman hailed it as correct and proper. As for MacCray, the charges were dropped.

For the purposes of this study, we make a special category for Phillips, Robles, MacCray, and others like them. In their cases we are not as certain of their innocence as we are in the cases that follow in detail, nor are we at all certain of their guilt. It is our view that these individuals were not given fair trials (a position upheld in the case of MacCray by the appeals court), and we ourselves are far from convinced of their guilt beyond a reasonable doubt.

Declared Innocent, and Still Incarcerated

Before we come to the numbers and some of the cases behind the numbers, let us look at the case of a man whose innocence was acknowledged by all parties to the proceedings—prosecution, sheriff, and judge—yet who remained in prison while the bureaucratic wheels of the criminal justice system ground slowly and absurdly.

The American criminal justice system is an Alice-in-Wonderland medley of intricacies, contradictions, and self-defeating propositions that even the superb imagination of a Kafka could not have surpassed. Among American judges there are many good minds, but by no means is there the general excellence found in the law schools or among the judiciary in England or Japan, for example, partly because the process by which judges become judges in most of the United States still has far more to do with politics than with merit. Prosecutors, attorneys general, district attorneys, and defense attorneys are not always highly competent, and their ethics, as the injustices we have examined show, are often deplorable, their actions sometimes even conspiratorial. The complex bureaucratic mechanisms often serve only the lawyers whose skills are required and whose profession enjoys a monopoly.

The backlogs on the court calendars in large cities grow like adolescents entering their growth spurts, but the growth spurts in crowded calendars never come to a halt. In this medley of the incomprehensible—including interminable postponements; convicts occasionally walking out of courtrooms purely by mistake and disappearing, never to be found again; wrong defendants pleading guilty to the wrong charges; and innumerable other signs of incredible breakdown—one becomes prepared for the conviction of innocents, the exoneration of the guilty, and sentences that differ markedly from one judge to another. But one is still not quite prepared for the case of Johnny Binder.

Binder was a black man, and the crime for which he was eventually wrongfully convicted was committed by a group of black people. He had one other factor in his life that linked him to those who robbed a store in Houston, Texas, and drove off with loot estimated at $400,000 in cash and valuable jewelry. The robbers used a yellow Cadillac similar to the one owned by Binder for their getaway. Only on these points did Binder's life and those of the criminals coincide: the color and make of the car, and the color of the skin.

Binder was in Dallas at the time the crime was committed. That is a considerable distance from Houston, as any Texan would know, but he was a resident of Houston. That he could establish his whereabouts in Dallas on the day the crime took place, and even at the almost exact time, gave him a sense of reassurance, although he was frightened when he read the description of the automobile used by the robbers. Having no criminal record whatsoever, knowing he was innocent, and possessing an airtight alibi, he discussed the matter of the automobile with his mother, who advised him to go to the police and explain the predicament. This he did, whereupon he was placed under arrest, charged with being one of the participants in the robbery.

There was a trial, and the similarity of the automobile seemed much more impressive to the all-white jury than the testimony concerning his presence in Dallas at the time of the crime, although the latter was substantiated by others and no effort on the part of an ardent prosecution could break it. There was still the matter of eyewitnesses to the crime: Some of them testified that they could recall Binder's presence as one of the robbers, others denied it. The defendant was able to take the stand in his own defense, something that can be done only with great risk by innocent people who have criminal records, because it offers the prosecution an opportunity to bring before the jury the purported evilness of the subject. On the stand, Binder made a good presentation of himself. Nonetheless, he was found guilty, and whether because of race or his failure to be contrite and admit the wrongdoing, or whether the fact that the robbers were armed made this a particularly heinous crime in the eyes of the judge, he was sentenced, as a first offender, to serve 18 years. He was taken off to prison while appeals were being made, and several appeals courts rejected his requests to have the verdict overturned or to have a new trial.

Johnny Binder spent 4 years in a Texas prison, and there was every likelihood that he would spend many more, for a person who is innocent and who persists in proclaiming his innocence is often regarded by parole boards as less "rehabilitated" than one who is indeed guilty, but contrite. In the latter part of 1983, Binder's attorneys uncovered evidence that a woman serving time in a California prison and two men who were also imprisoned, one in Louisiana, had committed the crime for which Binder had been convicted. There had been a report that one of the armed robbers was a woman, and when this convict was given a polygraph test (the accuracy of such tests is considered unreliable), the lie detector experts concluded that her story, namely, that Binder had not been involved in the crime, was the truth.

At a hearing before a Texas court, which took into consideration the original trial, the unbreakable alibi, the doubt of many eyewitnesses, and now the confession of one of the perpetrators, the judge stated without equivocation that she was convinced of Johnny Binder's innocence. But she could not free him or even grant him a new trial. To quote the judge, "This court is convinced, Mr. Binder, that the testimony given by Miss Terrell is true and correct and that you are in fact not involved." But justice has its peculiar ways in the United States, and it was patiently explained to Binder that he could not be granted a new trial because that remedy had already been denied by the Texas Court of Criminal Appeals. Binder returned to his prison cell, his innocence believed not only by his attorneys and by the judge who had conducted the hearing but also by the county district attorney and the county sheriff. While he was back in prison, these officers of the law petitioned for a pardon for Binder from the Texas Board of Pardons and Paroles.

In the meantime, unwilling to wait for the bureaucratic procedures that he felt would eventually free his client, Binder's attorney sought a writ of habeas corpus, which would free the innocent man immediately. "I don't understand," Binder was quoted as saying. "I was found innocent, but I'm still incarcerated." Technically—and the law can be very convoluted when it is bound up in its own technicalities—Binder had never been found innocent: that can be done only by a new verdict following a new trial or by some other route that would vacate the finding of guilt. He had not been "found innocent," he had been *declared* innocent by everyone on the law enforcement side of the case. And the writ of habeas corpus was denied; the attorney was told that this was not the proper and appropriate route to be taken when there is a claim for a new trial based on newly discovered evidence.

At that point a new force entered this story: the press. The *Houston Post* gave the case considerable space, ran editorials, and expressed its indignation concerning the inaction of a criminal justice system that kept a man incarcerated when literally everyone associated with the prosecution was now convinced that he was the wrong man. The public was now knowledgeable and indignant, but the Texas Board of Pardons and Paroles was taking no action.

Again, a peculiar twist occurred in this already strange case. Judge Kegans, who had heard the case after the California inmate made her confession and who had so firmly stated her belief both in Binder's innocence and in the fact that she could not free him, decided that although she did not have the legal right to free him on bond, she would do so nevertheless. In the interest of justice, she would violate the rules of the court. Freeing him on a $1,000 personal recognizance bond, she said, simply, "You go on home."

This was still not the end of the case, because Binder was free on bail only pending further action in the matter. A few days later, the Board of Pardons and Paroles recommended to the governor of Texas that he grant a full pardon to Johnny Binder. However, the board deliberately omitted from its recommendation that the pardon should be issued because of its belief that Binder was innocent. The difference between a full pardon with or without that stipulation could be enormous, for without such a stipulation of innocence, the fact of the conviction is not effaced: Binder would remain convicted of committing a felony and then pardoned after serving some 4 years or more in prison. If ever he were to be found guilty again, he could be treated as a two-time offender; if ever he were even accused again, the previous conviction would come back to haunt him. Not only that, but probably another factor, unmentioned, might have been in the minds of the board members: that Binder might sue and ask to be compensated for the time served and the pain and humiliation he and his family had suffered as a result of the wrongful conviction.

In one respect Binder's case is atypical: that he continued to remain in prison when everyone agreed that he was innocent. In another respect it is very typical: that conviction is generally not caused by one single defect in the system, but by a combination—the coincidence of the similarity of the automobile, the greater ease with which blacks are victimized by prejudice than are whites in our society, the unreliability of eyewitness identification, the failure of the prosecution to make a thorough check of alibi witnesses (a check that would have convinced the prosecutors that there was grave doubt as to the guilt of the accused), and the failure to make known to the defense, in violation of the ethics and canons of criminal law, that there were eyewitnesses who denied that Binder was one of the robbers. These are the types of issues that we shall look at in the more global picture of convicted innocents presented in the following chapters. What are the causes of wrongful convictions, and how can such events be prevented? How many people might still be in prison who are innocent, as we may or may not learn in the months or years ahead? How many people plead guilty in order to walk out of court and get a costly or a worrisome matter over with? What compensation does society owe to these victims? And what are the policy implications of all of this for the criminal justice system?

Note

1. This observation is shared even by the brilliant and passionate Alan Dershowitz (1983), who has won acquittals in some of the highest profile cases of the past 20 years: "I am not unique in representing guilty defendants. That is what most defense attorneys do most of the time. The Perry Mason image of the heroic defender of innocent victims of frame-ups or mistaken identification is television fiction. Occasionally truly innocent defendants are brought to trial; less frequently they are convicted. In some cases they have even been executed. But these cases—important as they are—are not the daily fare of the criminal lawyer" (p. xiv).

2

Causes Célèbres

Some of the cases of convicted innocents, and others where doubt remains concerning guilt, have been extensively discussed or debated (where doubt remains) for many years and will continue to be subjects of discussion whenever the issue of "guilt beyond a reasonable doubt" arises. Some of these cases elicit passionate advocates on both sides, where guilt or innocence remains a contested point. In cases where it is clear that the convicted persons were innocent beyond doubt, the discussion tends to focus more heavily on the question, How could this have happened? These cases become part of the history of a nation and, in some cases, rival other news events as some of the most sensational stories of given eras. In some cases, the personal tragedy borne by the innocent victim of a justice system gone awry overwhelms all else. In other cases, the incompetence or maliciousness of actors in the system stands out. In still others, the remarkable physical resemblance of the convicted innocent to the real perpetrator is striking, whereas in other cases the two bear little resemblance to each other. Some cases find their way into scholarly books, novels, or even movies, and writers of such works may or may not remain faithful to the facts of the cases. For various reasons, some of these cases become causes celébrès—the subjects of national or even international attention—and others fail to elicit more than passing interest; still others, of course, involve errors that are never even discovered.

The cases that form the substance of this chapter are those that, for various reasons, have grabbed the attention of the nation, sometimes the world. The subjects of our discussion are, almost without exception, people with few funds and no great following—few people interested in turning their travails into great political issues. Some have gone to their deaths, their innocence notwithstanding. Some have been on death row and escaped the executioner just in time. Some have languished for many years in prison before being exonerated by chance events or as a result of dogged struggles on the part of their families, other loved ones, journalists, attorneys, or even law enforcement officers whose consciences never quite permitted them to "close the book" on their cases. One (John Demjanjuk) was not even convicted and may not be entirely innocent, but we include his case because it is so controversial and because it illustrates the role of eyewitness identification. The Demjanjuk case is truly an international cause célèbre.

On far too many other occasions, when individuals are given terms of 1 to 3 or 5 years in prison, or even suspended sentences and probation, few believe in their innocence and even fewer care. Nonetheless, the unknown and forgotten convicted innocents have a great deal in common with the causes celébrès. Both are victims of the criminal justice system; they shed light on the shortcomings and machinations of that system; they open eyes—whether of a few or of the entire world—to the abuses and entanglements of the system, of the shame and the sham that it sometimes presents, of the enormous potential for injustice that can be imposed by those with absolute power. Finally, in a surprising number of instances, there are remarkable similarities among these cases: frame-ups, perjuries, cover-ups, intimidation, prejudice, and the enormous pressure on authorities not to admit error (and even to ratify the initial error) once it has been made. Sigmund Freud, the father of psychoanalytic theory, argued that we can learn a great deal about the normal by studying the pathological. By analogy, we believe that we can learn a great deal about our system of justice by analyzing injustice.

Just what are causes celébrès? The translation of the French word *cause* is actually closer to the English word *trial* than to the English use of *cause*.

Thus, the French phrase *causes celébrès,* literally translated, refers to famous, celebrated, or even notorious trials (although it has sometimes been used to refer to famous causes, for which people take up their banners and fight, and it is sometimes used to describe infamous crimes that did not result in trial, because there was no arrest). Not all of the great causes celébrès around which cases have been fought and struggles have raged have involved accused individuals whose innocence has been definitely established. But they are all of importance, because they demonstrate defects in the system of justice that cast dark clouds over the public's perception of the system's integrity and fairness.

One can trace such famous trials at least as far back as Socrates, who may never have lived except as a character in the dialogues of Plato. If subjected to the scrutiny of modern criminal jurisprudence, Socrates would not emerge as an innocent man, because in the eyes of the Athenian power holders and public, he did commit the crime of corrupting the youth of Athens. It can be more properly stated that Socrates' vision of corruption did not coincide with that of the authorities; in a sense, he may be seen as akin to Nelson Mandela in our own times, morally but not legally innocent, for righteousness was on his side. One may continue with the trial of Jesus, whose life is surrounded by so much myth and meaning that it is difficult to separate myth from history, or either from symbolism. Executed by crucifixion for the sins of man, or for preaching what the Roman powers declared to be heresy, a capital crime, even Jesus is not an exemplar of a convicted innocent—it was righteousness (or, in today's terms, "doing the right thing") that characterized his acts, not innocence of the charge of having violated the official "criminal code" in effect at that time.

The medieval era, the Dark Ages that marked the millennium between the triumph of Christianity and the first glimmer of light that was to become the Renaissance, were marked by countless executions of innocent people, but no single case became etched in the memory of humankind. During the Renaissance, when church and state were launching their historic struggle for hegemony, there was the trial of Galileo, again for heretical statements, and the heresy is not diminished by the veracity of those statements. Galileo challenged the legitimate and sovereign powers and then, when found guilty, publicly retracted the scientific findings that he had reported.

Closer to the genre of our studies are the Salem witch trials, created by hysteria, replete with prejudice, false accusations that some of the accusers might have believed to be true, and false confessions. During this period of colonial American history many innocent people, primarily women, were sent to their deaths although they were guiltless of the imaginary crimes for which they were placed on trial. When this period of mass hysteria eventually passed and peace returned to the community, it became apparent that the accused who had forfeited their lives had not done so entirely in vain: The memory of the witch-hunts remained an unpleasant reminder of the potential for injustice in the new nation that would soon be born. However, the memory of the events that took place in Salem was unable to protect the nation from such mistakes as the Palmer raids and the McCarthy era.

A Nineteenth-Century Case: The Dreyfus Affair

Among the causes célébrès the name of Alfred Dreyfus stands out, unparalleled for the upheaval that it brought about, for its repercussions not only in France but throughout much of the rest of the world. The events of the case have been skillfully and carefully analyzed, especially by Chapman (1955), Tuchman (1962), and Bredin (1986), on whose works we have relied a great deal in developing our own understanding of the case. On October 15, 1894, Dreyfus, a French artillery captain attached to the General Staff, was arrested on charges of having betrayed his country by selling military secrets to the Germans. The preceding September, a letter containing a list and descriptions of new artillery weapons used in the French army had somehow been taken from the office of the German military attaché in Paris and sent to the French War Office. The Statistical Section, which was the agency employing spies and in charge of counterespionage, received the document. That section was headed by Colonel Jean Conrad Sandherr, who was known, among other things, for his anti-Semitic views.

The document was passed to the chiefs of all the War Office departments. It occurred to the chief of the General Staff, after comparing the handwriting of several officers with that on the document, that there could be only one culprit—Captain Alfred Dreyfus, a probationer at the War Office, a Jew who was relatively wealthy, ambitious, and unpopular. On

November 1 of that year, an anti-Semitic newspaper, *La Libre Parole*, announced the arrest of Dreyfus. The accused was convicted of treason by a closed court martial on December 22. During the course of the trial, the court received as evidence a secret document prepared by the War Office. Dreyfus was degraded and sent to penal servitude on Devil's Island, off the coast of Guiana. Nearly all were convinced of Dreyfus's guilt, and the case seemed to be closed.

It was only the family of the convicted man, in particular his brother, who protested the conviction and were determined to bring about an exoneration and uncover the real traitor. Meanwhile, a new officer had been appointed to the counterespionage department—Major George Picquart. After reading a letter addressed to Walsin Esterhazi, a counter-espionage officer, Picquart suspected that Esterhazi might be another traitor. After all, in addition to the letter, Picquart had learned that a French officer was employed by the Germans—and Esterhazi fit the description of that officer. Picquart also compared Esterhazi's handwriting with that of the document used to convict Dreyfus, and was struck by the similarity. At first, Picquart believed that Dreyfus and Esterhazi were accomplices, fellow traitors. However, upon realizing that the handwriting on the document was Esterhazi's, he began to question Dreyfus's guilt.

Lieutenant Colonel Henry, a senior officer at the War Office, alarmed at Picquart's doubts and aware of the flimsy evidence used to convict Dreyfus, began to manufacture additional forgeries in an attempt to cover the fabricated evidence used to convict Dreyfus. Meanwhile, Dreyfus's brother, who became aware of Esterhazi's possible guilt, persuaded a senator of the need to revisit the case. On December 7, 1897, Esterhazi faced a court martial and was found not guilty.

The "Dreyfus affair," almost ignored in its early stages, was now creating considerable interest. A group of French officers and politicians who considered themselves "anti-Dreyfusards" viewed the attempt to exonerate Dreyfus and discredit the army as a Jewish conspiracy. Passion was aroused several days later when *L'Aurore* published an open letter written by Emile Zola to the president of the French Republic. Zola denounced the verdict as a crime against humanity and accused members of the General Staff of forgery and conspiracy. As a result of this advocacy, Zola was tried and found guilty of libel. He was persuaded to leave France in order to avoid imprisonment.

The election of 1898 brought to power a new government and, with it, a new minister of war. The new minister, known for his integrity, ordered a reexamination of the Dreyfus case. This investigation subsequently led to the conclusion that the crucial evidentiary document used to convict Dreyfus had in fact been forged, and that the actual culprit was Esterhazi. On September 29, the criminal chamber of France's highest court agreed to accept the case. Although the court did not have the power to declare Dreyfus innocent, it could overturn the court martial decision and ask for another trial. All was not over, however, as indicated by the fact that several cabinet members still believed Dreyfus was guilty (Bredin, 1986). It was not until July 1906 that Dreyfus was fully exonerated and Esterhazi found guilty of treason.

What caused this miscarriage of justice to occur? As in most cases of wrongful conviction we have analyzed, no single cause led to the conviction of Dreyfus. In fact, Chapman (1955), in his own analysis of the case, notes that the case arose in part due to a coincidence—the striking similarity in the handwriting of Dreyfus and Esterhazi. However, the fact that the officers at the French War Office were aware of the forgeries and the fabrication of evidence makes it clear that anti-Semitism played a major role in the conviction of Dreyfus. It was clearly a major contextual variable in the case. Although there was no direct linkage made at the time between Dreyfus's "guilt" and his being Jewish, it is clear that many found the idea of his guilt easier to accept because of the anti-Semitic context in which these events unfolded. Anti-Semitism was a political and social force that emerged in part as a result of tensions between classes and nations in nineteenth-century Europe. Fears and social conflicts resulted from industrialization, imperialism, and the power of money, as against the decline of the countryside and socialism. Anti-Semitism, under those circumstances, was a classic outlet; the Jews in France, as well as those living elsewhere, could be scapegoated and the attention deflected from the governing class.

Anti-Semitism in France is not restricted to the period of the Dreyfus case, as Zuccotti (1993) documents in a recent book titled *The Holocaust, the French, and the Jews.* In June 1940 (nearly half a century after Dreyfus's conviction), when the head of the new Vichy government requested an armistice, there were 330,000 Jews living in France, about

59% of whom were French citizens. More than 16,000 of the 195,000 Jews who were French citizens were murdered. The fate of those Jews who were not French citizens was even worse—nearly 65,000 of 135,000 were killed. The anti-Semitic legislation promulgated by the government and its acquiescence in Nazi persecution and execution reveal that such anti-Semitism was attributable to broader social and historical forces than simply the German Nazi influence.

Anti-Semitism is not, of course, confined to Europe. There are numerous examples of its effects on American justice. Perhaps the most egregious of all American cases influenced by anti-Semitism was that of Leo Frank, a Jewish businessman from Atlanta who in 1913 was convicted, based on perjured testimony, and sentenced to death for the murder of one of his employees, 13-year-old Mary Phagan. Outside the courthouse during the trial, crowds shouted "Hang the Jew!" Frank's sentence was commuted in 1915 by the governor of Georgia, who had serious doubts about Frank's guilt. When the commutation was announced, a frenzied mob chanting anti-Semitic slogans stormed the prison where Frank was confined, abducted him, and lynched him in Cobb County, Georgia. At the same time, another mob stormed the governor's mansion to protest the commutation. In the ensuing days, other Jews were attacked, and many fled the state (Dinnerstein, 1968).

Leo Frank finally received a posthumous pardon in 1986, a year after Alonzo Mann, a key witness, came forward to admit that as a 14-year-old, he had seen another man (not Frank) carrying the victim's body at the scene of the murder. He had not come forward at the time, he said, because his life had been threatened and his mother counseled silence. Jim Conley, the janitor who had been seen carrying the body and the probable perpetrator of the murder, had been a key witness against Leo Frank (Yant, 1991). The dynamics of the Frank case, and the anti-Semitic atmosphere in which it unfolded, reveal striking parallels to the Dreyfus tragedy just two decades earlier.

The Frank lynching was one of the earliest high-profile cases in 20th-century America, a century in which a number of causes célèbres stand out, not all of which have been decided to everyone's satisfaction. One of the most clear-cut, however, unfolded just 12 years after Leo Frank's hanging. This time, the state was Alabama and the issue was race.

The Scottsboro Boys

The ordeal for nine young black males began in 1927, when two white women were found illegally riding on a freight train with the nine black male teenagers. The women alleged that they had been raped. These allegations enraged many white Alabamians, who were further incensed when three white women from Birmingham were abducted, raped, and shot, allegedly by a black man. The sole survivor of the latter incident, Nell Williams, observed a man named Willie Peterson, whom she thought was her attacker, several weeks later and her brother detained the suspect. It turned out that Peterson did not match the description the woman had given police at the time of the crime. Furthermore, Peterson had a number of witnesses to support his alibi concerning his whereabouts at the time of the crime. The victim's brother, Dent Williams, apparently afraid that the "offender" might not be convicted, shot him. The gunshot wounds were not critical, and Peterson survived, only to be quickly convicted and sentenced to die in the electric chair. Like Leo Frank, Peterson would see his sentence commuted to life, but would die much sooner—in his case, due to tuberculosis. Dent Williams, the man who shot Peterson, was never indicted (Carter, 1969).

All nine of the young men who came to be known as the Scottsboro boys were tried and convicted by an all-white jury in a process that was somewhat analogous to an assembly line turning out widgets. All but one (the youngest) were sentenced to death. After many years of appeals, retrials, and reconvictions (replete with multiple violations of due process, racism, perjury, and other factors about which we have written), the nine young men spent a total of 104 years of their collective lives in prison for crimes that apparently never occurred. Most observers believe that the women who accused them were not raped at all, but concocted the story to explain why they had been in the company of "Negroes." Their rape allegations not only damaged the lives of the innocent defendants, but also increased skepticism concerning rape allegations, thus adding to the burden of all subsequent rape victims.

Some 50 years after this case began, the final surviving defendant, Clarence Norris, was granted an unconditional pardon by the state of Alabama, which cited extensive evidence that all nine defendants were, in fact, innocent (Yant, 1991). The particular combination of racism, the young age of the defendants, obvious due process violations, and the severe sentences handed out created a backlash of public sentiment throughout the United States. As with many of the other cases we have examined, both causes celébrès and less visible cases, more than one part of the system had broken down. Multiple errors, committed in a highly charged atmosphere (in this case, involving racism and public fear), combined to produce the tragic result. The convictions cannot be attributed to eyewitness error alone, though the initial identification set the process in motion. The web that was woven around the Scottsboro defendants included many architects. As a result, the Scottsboro case, in legal circles, has become synonymous with three albatrosses—racism, inadequate counsel (which we discuss in Chapter 3), and false rape allegations.

The Lindbergh Baby Kidnapping

Less than a decade after the infamous Scottsboro convictions, the attention of the nation, and much of the world, was focused on the kidnapping and murder of Charles Lindbergh, Jr., and the subsequent conviction and execution of a German immigrant carpenter, Bruno Richard Hauptmann, for this heinous crime. This remains a controversial case, in that there is not universal agreement that Hauptmann was innocent. Fortunately, the case has received extensive journalistic and scholarly attention over the years, including a recent book-length treatment by Ludovic Kennedy (1985a), an internationally acclaimed British author, who presents a compelling argument that Hauptmann, convicted and executed in 1936, never received a fair trial and was a convenient scapegoat, in part due to his German heritage at a time when Germans were very unpopular in the United States.

As virtually everyone knows, "Lucky Lindy" was a beloved figure in the United States because of his exploits as an aviator and his popular stand on political "isolationism." His wife, Anne Morrow Lindbergh, was the daughter of a wealthy and highly visible family. Hauptmann, on the other hand, was a German immigrant carpenter who had a criminal record—a convenient scapegoat who, following a 2-year nationwide and frenzied search for the abducted (and, it turned out, murdered) baby, was arrested, convicted, and executed for the "crime of the century," as some

referred to it. The case involved a grossly unfair series of police, prosecutorial, and judicial actions, including a circuslike trial conducted in a
hypercharged, nearly hysterical atmosphere, and a professionally inadequate defense attorney who kept Lindbergh's photograph on his desk,
worshipped the victim's father, and put on one of the weakest defenses
ever witnessed in a high-profile felony trial in the United States.

The Lindbergh/Hauptmann case vividly illustrates one of our major
findings—that wrongful conviction generally involves more than one
type of error and it is almost impossible to untangle the "interaction
effects" that generate such false positives. The elements that resulted in
this miscarriage of justice included prejudice, circumstantial evidence,
police and prosecutorial overzealousness in response to the pressure to
"get someone" and solve this high-profile crime against the child of a
beloved cultural icon and his esteemed wife, perjury, suppression of
potentially exculpatory evidence, intimidation of witnesses, and inadequate defense counsel. Even Governor Hoffman of New Jersey, who
offered Hauptmann the possibility of a life sentence in exchange for his
confession (Hauptmann refused), sent Hauptmann to his death while
reportedly believing that the man had been framed.

After an extensive reconstruction of this case, Ludovic Kennedy first
made a BBC documentary about it and then wrote his brilliant analysis,
The Airman and the Carpenter (1985a). Kennedy's reconstruction of the
events shows that Hauptmann was friends with a German immigrant and
con artist named Isidor Fisch, to whom Hauptmann entrusted some of his
own funds. Upon discovering that Fisch had died while visiting Germany,
Hauptmann opened a package Fisch had left with him and discovered that
it contained money. Unfortunately for Hauptmann, the money was part of
the ransom paid in the Lindbergh baby's kidnapping and included marked
bills. Hauptmann, apparently feeling he was entitled to this money (because Fisch had died and Hauptmann had no idea how to recover his own
funds that had been in Fisch's possession), naively and freely spent the
marked bills, leading the police directly to his door.

If Hauptmann did not kidnap and kill the baby, the question remains,
Who did? Kennedy (1985a) reports that the ransom note may have been
written by someone from either Austria or southern Germany and that
when Hauptmann first met Fisch, Fisch was in the company of an Aus-
trian. Also, Kennedy argues that Fisch's partners in the bogus Knicker-
bocker Pie Company, Charles Schleser and Joe DeGrasi, should have been

more carefully investigated. As in many other cases we have analyzed (nearly all less visible than this one), the apprehension of a "likely suspect," especially one with a previous criminal record, like Hauptmann, often shifts the entire investigative process to one based on deductive, rather than inductive, logic. The "rules of the game" shift toward proving the prime suspect's guilt (get someone, clear the books, and move on to the next case), rather than keeping an open mind and pursuing leads to other suspects as well. The problem with this is that by the time the error is discovered, the leads to the real offender (witnesses, physical evidence, and the offender him- or herself) have often evaporated. It is extremely difficult for police and prosecutors to recover from such major false starts.

How can prosecutors allow such travesties to occur? According to the canons of ethics that apply to their profession, they are supposed to pursue justice, not only convictions. Alan M. Dershowitz (1983), professor of law at Harvard University and one of the nation's most brilliant appellate attorneys, observes:

> Prosecutors are supposed to be interested in justice: the motto on the wall of the Justice Department proclaims that the government "wins its point whenever justice is done." But in real life, many prosecutors reverse the motto and believe that justice is done whenever the government wins its point. (p. xvi)

But even if prosecutors feel the pressure to convict and sometimes take shortcuts to "get their man," surely the judges, being more insulated and protected from public pressure, are there to ensure fairness and to scrutinize the process. Again, Dershowitz (1983) offers a cynical view of some judges, based on many years of direct involvement in the system:

> Many see themselves as part of the system of law enforcement, as adjuncts to the police and prosecutors. They want to make sure that criminals are convicted and sent away. Even if the law requires acquittal, many judges will do everything within their lawful power—and some things beyond it—to convict defendants who they believe should be in jail. . . . I have been more disappointed by judges than by any other participants in the criminal justice system. That is partly because I, like so many others, expected so much of these robed embodiments of the law. (pp. xvii-xviii)

As for Hauptmann, his widow, Anna, fought for his complete exoneration until the moment she died (October 10, 1994, at age 95). The final chapter of this case is still being written. Anna Hauptmann's attorney, Robert Bryan, believes that newly discovered documents, which had been stored at the home of former Governor Hoffman, will completely exonerate Bruno Richard Hauptmann. And the documents have generated yet another controversy. Fingerprints attributed to the Lindbergh baby are included in the documents, and a man has come forward claiming that he, in fact, is the son of the Lindberghs, and that the body recovered by police was actually that of an unidentified infant.

The Sad Saga
of Isidore Zimmerman

Those causes célébrès. that involve clear-cut evidence of wrongful conviction can all be described as genuine personal tragedies. They are certainly devastating to the lives of the convicted innocents, even when they are exonerated and freed from prison, or even spared death. One of the saddest cases we know of is that of Isidore Zimmerman, wrongfully convicted in New York in 1937, just a year after the execution of Bruno Richard Hauptmann. Zimmerman, at the time a young hotel doorman, was convicted and sentenced to die for providing guns that were later used in the murder of a police detective. Even though Zimmerman was not at the scene of the crime, he spent 24 years in prison and, in 1939, his head shaved, his trousers slit, and his last meal consumed, came within 2 hours of execution at Sing Sing before his sentence was commuted to life.

It took Zimmerman more than two decades after that commutation to convince the world that he had been innocent all along. The case involved perjury by a key witness (perjury that was known to the assistant district attorney), prosecutorial overzealousness, and unethical conduct. After serving 24 years in prison and having his conviction reversed in 1962, Zimmerman set out to gain compensation for his ordeal—a process that would take 20 more years of his life. As is the case in most states, Zimmerman was required to obtain a special bill from the New York State Legislature before he was allowed to sue for compensation.[1] In addition to the deprivation of his liberty for a crime he did not commit, Zimmerman lost the use of his right eye during a prison beating—factors that were taken into account in setting his compensation at $1 million, which amounted to approximately $660,000 after legal fees were deducted (Yant, 1991, p. 149).

What happened next can only be described as a compound tragedy. After more than four decades spent in prison, in clearing his name, and in obtaining some monetary compensation (a net of $27,500 per year of imprisonment), Zimmerman, according to his attorney, bought a new car, took a trip to the Catskills, and, within 4 months of receiving his monetary award, died prematurely of a heart attack at the age of 66 (Yant, 1991, p. 149). One can only speculate as to what role his wrongful conviction and 24 years in prison may have played in shortening his life.

Randall Dale Adams:
Injustice in Dallas

Imagine you are dreaming: You have been accused of murder. You have never seen or heard of the victim. You have no knowledge of where or when it occurred. . . . The words of the prosecutors echo in your mind as they describe what will happen to you: "they strap you down . . . your eyeballs explode . . . your fingernails and toenails pop off . . . you bleed from every orifice of your body." The jury files into the room. . . . The bailiff reads the verdict: Guilty! Finally you awaken. You are drenched in perspiration, but you are filled with relief to realize that it was just a dream. But for me, it was a real-life nightmare. (Adams, 1991, pp. xiii-xiv)

This harrowing description, excerpted from the prologue to Randall Dale Adams's own remarkable book, *Adams v. Texas* (1991), allows one to imagine what it would be like to be convicted and sentenced to death for murdering someone one had never met. Adams lived that experience and much more at the hands of a justice system gone awry in Dallas. For readers of Adams's book, or viewers of Errol Morris's prize-winning documentary re-creation of the case, *The Thin Blue Line* (1988), the case is one they will never forget; nor would most of them ever have imagined it could happen in America.

Adams, a lifelong resident of Columbus, Ohio, had been traveling with his brother, Ray, through the usually warm South in an attempt to get some relief from his arthritis. They had decided to change their final destination from Florida to southern California, and were working for a while in Texas on the way. The night of November 28, 1976, however, was a cold one in the Dallas area and Adams ran out of gas about a mile from his ultimate destination, the motel where he and his brother were staying. Finding an empty plastic milk container in the trunk, he tried to buy gas at a Sinclair station, but was told that it was against the law to dispense gas into that type of container and that the attendant had no other container. Just as Adams was about to start walking to another gas station, a young man pulled up and offered him a ride. Adams accepted, a decision that, although he could not have foreseen it, would turn out to be the worst of his life. The young driver was David Harris, who, later that night, was to murder a Dallas police officer and frame Adams for the crime.

David Harris had stolen a neighbor's car and his father's gun the day prior to the murder of the police officer. After Harris picked up Adams and helped him get gas, Adams reciprocated by spending the rest of the day with him, including going to a drive-in movie theater and promising to help him find work. Although Harris claimed to be an electrician and Adams knew of no jobs for electricians, he believed he could help Harris find work at his own job site. After returning to the motel room he shared with his brother, Adams went to bed. At 12:38 a.m., Officers Robert Wood and Teresa Turko were just leaving a Burger King restaurant in west Dallas when they spotted a car driving with only its parking lights on. Wood, who was driving the police car, turned on his flashers and stopped the car. Then, without calling in the license number of the car (standard operating procedure), Officer Wood approached the driver, apparently to remind him to use his headlights (Wood left his citation book in the police car). After all, this would be a minor violation; indeed, it occurs frequently, especially when a driver has just left a well-lighted area, where headlights were unneeded. The failure of a police officer to call in a license number is also more common than one might think, because if things are busy there can be significant delays before information gained from a license plate check is relayed to the officer in the field. In any event and for whatever reason, Officers Wood and Turko took what turned out to be a fatal shortcut, and Wood unknowingly approached a man who had stolen a car and had a nine-shot, .22 caliber pistol loaded with hollow-point bullets in the front seat. Harris shot Wood six times, continuing to shoot even after the officer fell to the ground. Wood was taken to Parkland Hospital's emergency department, where, like President Kennedy 13 years earlier, he was pronounced dead.

Nearly a month later, Adams was arrested at gunpoint at his job site, taken downtown, and subjected to what he describes as a prolonged, physically exhausting interrogation, during which he was permitted no telephone calls (thus, no attorney), no food, no water, and no rest breaks, while the police took turns questioning him. Finally frustrated at their inability to crack Adams, the Dallas police brought in their top interrogator, the last man to question Lee Harvey Oswald before he was killed, Detective Sergeant Gus Rose. According to Adams's book, Rose attempted to get him to sign a confession and, when he refused, Rose

> returned a few minutes later. This time he held a gun in his hand, and he tossed it onto the table in front of me, commanding, "Look at that." . . . "Pick the son of a bitch up and look at it!" Did he want my fingerprints on it? Did he want me to appear armed, so that he could shoot me in "self-defense?" I replied as calmly as I could, "No sir, I will not touch that thing." . . . Rose pulled his service revolver . . . pointed it at my forehead, and cocked it. "I ought to blow your shit away," he said. (Adams, 1991, p. 28)

Eventually, Adams signed a vague statement that ended with a sentence he would come to regret: "I do not remember anything after I took a right on Inwood until I was turning left on Fort Worth Avenue" (pp. 29-30). Fatigued, he wanted to get his ordeal over with so he could eat, drink, and rest. The statement gave the authorities just the kind of flexibility they felt they needed to convict him. It was immediately labeled a "confession" and was used later to argue that Adams did not want to remember what happened at that point, because that is when the murder occurred. The next day, hoping to convince everyone of the truth, Adams agreed to take a polygraph exam. What he did not realize is the frequency with which polygraph "evidence" has contributed to wrongful conviction, not necessarily in its use in the courtroom but as intimidation to confess. Adams reports that his polygrapher administered two "inconclusive" exams before indicating that Adams struck out on the third try, thus adding to the evidence of this procedure's unreliability.

Adams was prosecuted by First Assistant District Attorney Doug Mulder, who had a reputation for winning and for obtaining the maximum penalties possible. He worked for the Dallas District Attorney's Office, then headed by Henry Wade (perhaps best known for *Roe v. Wade,* 1973). About Henry Wade, the *ABA Journal* would later say:

> He was a mighty figure who brooked no dissent and made no apologies. He judged his prosecutors, it is said, on their won-lost records: They were given raises and promotions according to their success in obtaining criminal convictions. According to those who worked under Wade, the DA *never questioned their methods* in obtaining guilty verdicts. ("Crime and Punishment," 1989, p. 52; emphasis added)

The *ABA Journal*'s cover for that issue boldly proclaimed, "WIN AT ANY COST? Dallas DA Under Siege," and the feature article focused on the exoneration of Randall Dale Adams as symptomatic of a pathological organizational culture in the Dallas D.A.'s office, one that continued into the administration of Wade's successor, John Vance. The journal cited criticism by judges, defense attorneys, and even former prosecutors that Vance "has not abandoned his predecessor's bankrupt philosophy of winning by any available means" ("Crime and Punishment," 1989, p. 53). Even after Adams's conviction had been set aside unanimously by the Texas Court of Appeals in March 1989, in a ruling that included sharp criticism of the Dallas D.A.'s Office, Vance's office wanted to retry Adams.

One can appreciate the seriousness of this problem only when one is forced to contemplate the following question: What could possibly motivate a prosecutor's office, knowing that the state's key witnesses had lied and having been censured by the state appellate court, to want to retry a man who had been framed, imprisoned for 12½ years, confined to death row for 3½ years, and was only 72 hours away from execution at one point? A D.A.'s office capable of this, it should come as no surprise, proved capable of convicting a series of innocent defendants, including Lenell Geter and Joyce Ann Brown, whose cases also attracted national media attention.

Later in this book, we shall present survey data indicating that the percentage of felony cases resulting in wrongful conviction is believed to be small. However, the evidence from Dallas suggests that this series of highly publicized wrongful convictions, instead of representing an atypical "blip" in a time-series analysis, may in fact represent instead the proverbial tip of the iceberg, given that office's "win at all costs" philosophy. One can only hope that the tragic events surrounding the discredited Dallas D.A.'s Office will serve to remind other prosecutors of their foremost obligation, which is neither to get reelected nor to win, but rather to seek justice. Otherwise, who could blame judges and jurors in Dallas if they are more reluctant to indict and convict citizens accused by an office whose morally and ethically reprehensible actions have caused it to be so highly criticized, even by such a respected, conservative publication of the legal profession as the *ABA Journal?*

As for the classification of this case in terms of errors, it illustrates once again that multiple errors occurred to produce system failure. David Harris, the real murderer, obviously offered perjured testimony as a key witness for the state in order to save himself. But his lie should have been overcome by good, solid, *inductive* investigative work. After all, Harris, who was a juvenile, had an extensive record and had bragged about the killing to some friends. There were plenty of investigative leads in that direction (including the fact that Harris had engaged in a crime spree on the day of the murder), had they been seriously pursued by the Dallas authorities and had such information been allowed by the judge (who prevented the jury from hearing about Harris's crime spree). The overzealousness on the part of the police in attempting to get a "cop killer" quickly, although understandable, contributed to the error; so did the prosecution's overzealousness and unethical behavior; so did some of the judicial rulings in the case, which did not really permit Adams's original defense attorneys to enjoy a level playing field. These factors, added to the fact that the real killer was the state's star witness and other witnesses lied as well, were insurmountable obstacles, even for one who was innocent of the charge and had a completely clean record and an honorable discharge from the military.

Why did the authorities go after Adams rather than Harris? Although no one really knows the answer to that question, Adams's own insight centers on how he was viewed by those authorities: To them he was

an outsider, a blue-collar worker new to Texas who presented them with the image of a long-haired pot-smoking "hippie." Another factor was the Texas political climate . . . demanding that someone should die in retaliation for Officer Wood's death. Because of his youth, David Harris could not be executed for murdering a police officer. On the other hand, a twenty-eight-year-old whom the judge himself described as a "drifter" was a prime candidate for the electric chair. . . . If the prosecution blamed me, it had a witness who said he was sitting in the passenger's seat at the time. If it chose Harris, it had no witness. (Adams, 1991, pp. 58-59)

So the prosecutors chose Adams as their target, which gave them Harris as a witness. To buttress the case, still weak, they produced three witnesses on the last day of the trial who were willing to swear that they had driven past the scene of the crime and that Adams was the bushy-haired man they had seen in the car that night. Adams's attorney, after hearing rumors that the three "surprise" witnesses had lied to collect part of the reward money offered to solve Officer Wood's murder, discovered that only one of the three affidavits had been signed prior to Adams's arrest, and that one had described the suspect as being either a light-complexioned African American or a Mexican (Adams is white). The other two affidavits had been produced after Adams's arrest and after the publication of his photograph and the publication of Harris's version of the story. The judge, again, would not permit the jury to know this information, which would have helped the defense's case.

Prosecutor Mulder's emotional closing statement was calculated to play on the jury's sympathy for the slain officer, even further distracting them from the facts of the case:

You know, being a soldier in this war on crime is not looked upon with the same patriotic fervor that there once was. . . . But you see, the dead are buried just the same. The war goes on. . . . Who protects the police officers? Who picks up their banner when they fall in battle . . . ? . . . Don't give this man a life sentence when he has earned death. . . . And I ask you don't turn your back on Robert Wood, don't break the faith with Robert Wood. (quoted in Adams, 1991, pp. 125-126)

During their deliberations, the jurors asked the judge's permission to visit the scene of the crime to assess firsthand the lighting conditions. This request indicated, of course, their concerns about the last-minute witnesses' claims that they saw Adams in the car that night, even though they were quite some distance away. Request denied. Justice denied. The testimony of the three lying witnesses stood, and Adams fell. Guilty as charged.

Next came the penalty phase, in which the jury had to determine whether Adams would receive a life sentence or the death penalty. Adams had been interviewed by two psychiatrists, one of whom was the infamous "Dr. Death," Dr. James Grigson. Grigson earned his nickname for helping send so many defendants to their deaths by testifying (after only cursory examinations) that they were sociopaths beyond hope of rehabilitation who presented continuing danger to society. In fact, Grigson's lack of professionalism became so well known that he would eventually be the subject of criticism by the U.S. Supreme Court, the ACLU, and the American Psychiatric Association—all within one week. He testified that Adams, whom he had seen for 20 minutes, was without remorse (a difficult feeling to have when one is innocent) and would likely kill again if given the chance. He and prosecutor Mulder got their wish later that day when Adams was sentenced to death by electrocution (Yant, 1991, pp. 27-28).

Adams's defense attorney filed a motion for a new trial, based on information that two of the late witnesses had lied to obtain reward money and to have charges dropped against one of their daughters (the charges were dropped just two days after Adams was found guilty). Motion denied. Justice denied.

It was not until 1980, when the U.S. Supreme Court concluded that Adams's jury had been improperly selected, that the injustices of Adams's case began to be addressed by the system. And it was just 72 hours before his scheduled execution that Adams won a stay ordered by Justice Lewis Powell. When the full Supreme Court finally heard the arguments in the case, the decision was clear to all but one of the justices. The vote was eight to one in favor of remanding Adams's case for retrial. The lone dissenting justice, who, observers reported, seemed not even to listen attentively and whose vote could have sent the innocent Adams to his death, was William Rehnquist, who would later become chief justice of the U.S. Supreme Court. The governor of Texas commuted Adams's sentence, probably to avoid the possibility of an acquittal if a new trial were held.

Nonetheless, Adams's request for a new trial was ultimately granted by District Judge Larry Baraka. That trial never occurred, because by then the documentary *The Thin Blue Line* (originally intended to focus on James "Dr. Death" Grigson) and national media attention had made it clear to the world that Adams had been framed in Dallas. The witnesses who had helped convict Adams had all been discredited, and the prosecution reluctantly decided that it had no recourse but to let Adams go. He was free for the first time in more than 12 years.

What was it like to be imprisoned for 12½ years for killing a police officer? In a recent lecture on the Ohio State University campus, Adams (1993) provided the answer:

> I have a nephew who is an Ohio State [Highway] Patrolman. . . . So here I am accused, similarly, of killing my nephew. To live inside a penitentiary . . . everybody that I respect—law enforcement, correctional officers—they're looking at me: "You're a cop killer!" That's not a nice look! All the people that I disrespect—the rapists, the killers—[are saying]: "You've been on death row, convicted of killing a cop, doing life! . . . The people that I respect, hate me; the people that I don't respect, respect me. It was a strange situation. . . . The one thing that saved me was my family—their love, their support.

Adams's mother, Mildred, a wonderful woman of modest means but great love for and faith in her son, lost her home and her life's savings—even sacrificed the money for her blood pressure medication when necessary to help free Randall from prison and from death—but she feels it was all worth it to stop the injustice in Dallas (Adams, 1991, pp. 220, 346). Randall's brother, Ray, with whom he shared the motel room on that fateful night in Dallas, disappeared from the face of the earth in 1979, and only recently has the family heard from him again. Adding to the family's concern was the fact that he did not even bother to pick up his last check from his employer at the time. Randall knows that it troubled his brother greatly that he could not honestly say what time Randall returned to the motel that night, because Ray was asleep. Ray chose not to lie, but he wished he could have done more at the time to help his brother's defense.

Former prosecutor Mulder left the Dallas D.A.'s Office in 1981 and established a prosperous law practice in Dallas, specializing in criminal defense—especially the defense of wealthy clients. He was once asked what might have happened if he had been Adams's attorney, instead of his prosecutor. He reportedly replied, "I'd have gotten him off. There's no doubt in my mind" (Adams, 1991, p. 346). For Mulder, it was obviously *winning* that was important.

As for David Harris, he virtually confessed to the murder of Officer Wood while being interviewed by Errol Morris for *The Thin Blue Line* and committed many more crimes after framing Adams. It is known that in addition to his crime spree that day, he later had a series of arrests for minor crimes; served 8 months in confinement at Ft. Leavenworth for violently assaulting his commanding officer in Germany; committed a series of burglaries and an armed robbery in 1978; stole a car and committed a spree of robberies and burglaries in California (where he attempted to shoot a police officer, but the gun misfired); was convicted of armed robbery and kidnapping (and tried to blame a hitchhiker, but was sentenced to 6 years at San Quentin); and, following parole, broke into an apartment back in Texas, kidnapped a woman, and murdered the woman's boyfriend. In 1986, David Harris was sentenced to death (Yant, 1991, pp. 30-31). The many violent crimes he committed after killing Officer Wood stand as vivid and sobering evidence in support of one of our main contentions: that wrongful conviction is not just a "liberal" issue concerning the rights of suspects, but also a public safety issue. Every wrongful conviction enables the real offender to continue victimizing others.

In the epilogue to his book, Adams (1991) says this about Harris:

> David Harris remains on death row at the Ellis unit. I wish him no good luck, but neither do I wish him harm. Whether he is executed or dies of old age in a prison cell is of little consequence to me now, but I know this much: I could never be the one to twist the valve that sent lethal chemicals into his veins. (p. 347)

This statement reveals much about Randall Dale Adams's character. As for Adams himself, he is still putting his life back together. It has not been easy. His income has included a job in his hometown of Columbus, Ohio, and proceeds from his book and from lectures. He has had to readjust to life outside prison, which is never easy. But given what he has been through, he is remarkably free of bitterness and cynicism, as evidenced by his comments concerning Harris and his acknowledgment to the jurors in his case:

> I thank the members of the jury who condemned me to death in 1977. Recently, several of them have commented to the press that, if they had been allowed to hear all of the pertinent evidence, they would have found me not guilty. I hold no malice in my heart for them; they were victims, too. (Adams, 1991, p. x)

Randall Adams is still struggling to put his life back together and exorcise the personal "demons" that his ordeal created.

As we have noted, the Adams case was only the most highly publicized of a series of wrongful convictions emanating from the Dallas District Attorney's Office. Although our study indicates that many wrongful convictions involve defendants with prior records, we discuss in this book a number of errors involving defendants with absolutely no criminal records. In addition to Randall Adams's death sentence, the Dallas County D.A.'s Office won convictions and life sentences in the cases of Lenell Geter and Joyce Ann Brown, neither of whom had prior criminal records. And later in the book, we present the tragic case of Steve Titus, wrongfully convicted in Seattle despite having a spotless record.

But first, back to Dallas, where Lenell Geter, a college-educated, 24-year-old black engineer, had a good job at E-Systems, a local military/ electronics firm. Geter's place of employment was Greenville, a suburban Dallas community that, as recently as the late 1960s, had a sign at the city limits that proclaimed: "The Blackest Land—The Whitest People" ("Some Doubt," 1983; cited in Yant, 1991, pp. 15-16). In 1982, there had been a series of armed robberies in suburban communities, including Greenville. An elderly woman in Greenville thought it was suspicious that Geter had a habit of hanging around a local park (he went there on his lunch hour to read and feed the ducks). A moral entrepreneur who apparently saw herself as protecting her white community from this suspicious black man, she passed Geter's license plate number on to the police. Subsequently, Geter's photo was shown to a number of robbery victims and, finally, he was "chosen" as the robber of a Kentucky Fried Chicken store, arrested, charged, and jailed.

Geter says that his attorney spent most of his time trying to persuade him to plead guilty to a lesser charge—to "deal" with the prosecutor's office. Geter, a religious and highly principled man, was offended by the very idea of pleading guilty when he was innocent. Several of Geter's white coworkers volunteered to testify that he was at work when the crime occurred and could not possibly have been the robber, but the attorney's lack of preparation and the judge's refusal to grant additional time resulted in these key witnesses' never being heard. Despite Geter's perfect record and the lack of any physical evidence linking him to the crime, he was convicted by an all-white jury and sentenced to life in prison. Further, Geter's attorney did not make the deadline required for filing for a retrial. Geter's loyal coworkers stood by him, however, and, outraged at the conviction of a man they had been with 50 miles away at the time of the crime, they raised money for his legal appeal. Finally, after extensive national and local media exposure of Geter's frame-up (including a featured segment on CBS's *60 Minutes*) and the arrest of another suspect in the robbery, the charges against Geter were dropped and he was permitted to go on with his life, after spending 14 months in prison. Following his release, the *New York Times* editorialized:

The criminal justice system works poorly enough for blacks in America, but in the case of Lenell Geter, it hardly worked at all. . . . His freedom depended more on the interest shown by his friends and by the press—good fortune not necessarily shared by everyone caught in the system. Mr. Geter may feel relief. Dallas County's officials should not. ("The Bad and Good Luck," 1984)

Actually, Dallas County's officials didn't have much time for relief. It is often alleged that some prosecutors in the Dallas County D.A.'s Office used to say (perhaps in "humor"), "Anybody can convict a guilty man; it takes a real prosecutor to convict an innocent one" ("Wrongful Conviction," 1989). If that was ever, even jokingly, a benchmark of success, the Dallas D.A.'s Office appeared to lead the nation in the 1980s. Besides Geter and Adams, a number of other innocent persons were wrongfully convicted by the Dallas D.A.'s Office during the 1980s and early 1990s. Within a single year, beginning in 1989, four such individuals were exonerated after serving up to 10 years in prison (Yant, 1991, p. 38).

Perhaps the best known of these injustices was that suffered by Joyce Ann Brown.

In 1989, Brown, like Geter and Adams before her, was freed from prison primarily by intense media exposure of the injustice she suffered, again including a feature story on *60 Minutes.* She had been convicted in 1980 for armed robbery and served more than 9 years of her life sentence before it was discovered that a key prosecution witness committed perjury during her trial. The robbery for which Brown was convicted occurred on May 6, 1980, when two women forced a fur store owner and his wife to stuff furs into plastic trash bags. One of the robbers shot the owner to death despite his pleas and then shot at, but missed, the owner's wife. The wife then told the robber that she had only a few weeks to live, due to terminal cancer. The robber reportedly replied, "We'll just let you suffer" ("Wrongful Conviction," 1989).

The robbers had used a getaway car that had been rented by a woman named Joyce Ann Brown. Even though it turned out that the Joyce Ann Brown who had rented the car was from Denver, a Dallas vice officer knew a local prostitute named Joyce Ann Brown and reported this to the investigators, who then added her photo to their montage. Ala Danziger, the wife of the slain furrier, picked Brown's photo as one of the two robbers. In addition to Danziger's identification of Brown, Dallas prosecutors had the word of Brown's cell mate, Martha Jean Bruce, that Brown had confessed to the crime while they shared a cell.

Even though jailhouse informants' testimony should be strongly suspect (especially where inducements such as dropped or reduced charges are involved), and even though four of Brown's coworkers (like Geter's) testified that she was at work with them at another fur store three miles away from the robbery at the time of the crime, Brown was convicted and sentenced to a life term. However, it turned out that the informant had previously lied to the police, a fact that had not been made known to the defense. Prosecutors insisted they were unaware of this fact but that they "should have known" and should have informed the defense ("Wrongful Conviction," 1989). The charges against Brown were dropped on February 14, 1990 (Yant, 1991, p. 39).

This Dallas trilogy, along with other wrongful convictions emanating from the Dallas District Attorney's Office, suggests that organizational culture may play an important role in setting the climate for such errors.

Has Dallas produced a higher percentage of errors than other major urban prosecutors' offices? Or have Dallas's mistakes simply received more intense national publicity? There is no way to answer this question accurately, because no reliable comparative statistics are kept on wrongful conviction. However, the data that are available in Texas seem to suggest that wrongful conviction has been a serious problem in Dallas for at least several decades, even before the series of cases described above:

> The Court of Criminal Appeals does not compile such statistics . . . but two studies by Dallas newspapers in the 1960s and 1970s showed that Dallas County had the state's highest reversal rate. Records from the state appeals court show that 14 of the 30 death penalty convictions from Dallas County that have been reviewed by appeals courts since 1973 have been reversed. Most were overturned because of improper jury selection and improper testimony from Dr. James Grigson, a Dallas psychiatrist nicknamed "Dr. Death" for his pro-prosecution views. ("Prosecution Style Blamed," 1989, p. 39A)

Another basis for reversals is improper arguments made before juries, and one review of Texas appellate court reversals from the mid-1960s to the mid-1970s indicates that more than a third of all such reversals involved cases from Dallas County. One might assume that such reversals would be sufficient cause for disciplining the offending prosecutor, but when asked if he believed that was the case in the Dallas D.A.'s Office, the district attorney of Harris County (Houston) replied: "Our perception was they were rewarded for it. They were made first assistant for it" ("Prosecution Style Blamed," 1989, p. 39A).

If organizational culture contributes to the positive accomplishments of organizations, as argued in management and leadership books such as *In Search of Excellence* (Peters & Waterman, 1982), it is also clearly the case that leadership and organizational culture can help produce negative outcomes and, ultimately, discredit the "product" of the organization. In discussing values and their place in organizational culture, Schein (1985) notes:

> As the values begin to be taken for granted, they gradually become beliefs and assumptions and drop out of consciousness, just as habits

become unconscious and automatic. . . . *A group can learn that the holding of certain beliefs and assumptions is necessary as a basis for maintaining the group.* (p. 16; emphasis added)

We will have more to say on the role of leadership and organizational culture in Chapter 6, where we discuss the public policy implications of this study.

"Ivan the Terrible," or a Terrible Case of Mistaken Identity?

A recent international cause célèbre that captured the world's attention involved controversial identification of a now 75-year-old retired auto-worker, John Demjanjuk of Cleveland, Ohio, as "Ivan the Terrible," a Nazi concentration camp guard and war criminal. We include this case here because it is truly a cause célèbre on the world's stage, and it vividly illustrates many of the problems inherent in the reliance on eyewitness identification, especially long after the crime in question. Whether or not Demjanjuk is ever convicted of any war crime, his will remain an international cause célèbre; his case will be raised whenever people discuss eyewitness testimony and its reliability.

Our summary of the case is based on legal documents and the work of Teicholz (1990). On the morning of February 16, 1987, the first trial of a Nazi war criminal held in Israel since the trial of Adolf Eichman (1961) began in Jerusalem (*State of Israel v. Ivan [John] Demjanjuk,* 1986). Demjanjuk was deported from the United States and charged with volunteering for the German SS and Security Police. It was alleged that he underwent training in the German training camp at Trawniki, Poland, where those trained became proficient in the arts of hanging and torturing civilians. From March 1943, he allegedly served with an SS unit in the town of Sobibor, Poland, and, beginning in October 1943, as a guard in the concentration camp at Flossenberg, Germany. He was charged with having participated in the mass executions of Jews at the Sobibor death camp.

The trail leading to Demjanjuk began in 1975, when the U.S. Immigration and Naturalization Service (INS) received a list of possible Ukrainian

Nazi collaborators at large in the United States. Demjanjuk's name was among them, and he was listed as having been a guard at Sobibor, an extermination camp a hundred miles south of Treblinka. The list was compiled by Michael Hanusiak, an editor of the *Ukrainian Daily News,* a pro-Soviet newspaper published in New York. Hanusiak also was a member of the Society for Cultural Exchange, a Soviet organization that promotes contact between the United States and the Ukraine. That organization granted him the access and contacts necessary to conduct research in the Soviet Union concerning Nazi collaborators who might be at large in the United States.

In the Soviet Union, Hanusiak browsed through newspaper archives and met with Soviet journalists, Polish attorneys, and editors of Soviet and Ukrainian newspapers. By the mid-1970s, he had compiled a list of 70 alleged Nazi collaborators living in the United States. A serious investigation was launched by the INS, and it was verified that Demjanjuk was living with his wife and children in Cleveland, Ohio. Material that contained photos and other information was assigned to Miriam Radiwker, an investigator in the special unit of the Israeli police devoted to the investigation of Nazi crimes. Radiwker reviewed the INS files and immediately took steps to locate Holocaust survivors who could identify at least two of the people described in the files, Fedorenko and Demjanjuk. The Nazi war crimes unit maintained photo albums of suspects, called *photospreads,* cataloged by nationality. Photospreads are an investigative tool similar to American police mug shot albums. Demjanjuk's 1951 visa photo and Fedorenko's 1949 visa photo were included in the photospread, pasted under the label "Ukrainian." Radiwker, who had previously worked with survivors of the Treblinka death camp, intended to locate some of the survivors and ask if they could identify anyone in the photospread.

The first potential witness who came to Radiwker's office was Eugen Turovsky. There are two conflicting versions of what happened next. The prosecution contends that Turovsky browsed through the photospread and, when he came to the third page, pointed to Demjanjuk's photo and said, "That's Ivan of Treblinka" (a mistake, because information indicated that Demjanjuk was at Sobibor, not Treblinka). The defense version of what happened is slightly different—that Turovsky first identified another Nazi criminal, Fedorenko, and did not identify the photo of Demjanjuk.

In any event, Radiwker decided to summon Turovsky once again the following morning, at which time, apparently assisted by some hints from Radiwker, he identified "Ivan."

Next, Radiwker summoned Avraham Goldfarb and asked him to view the photos. Goldfarb had built the large gas chamber at Treblinka, and he found Demjanjuk's photo familiar. However, when confronted with the information that Demjanjuk had been at Sobibor and Trawniki, he was unable to confirm this. The third witness was Eliahu Rosenberg, also a Treblinka survivor. When the Ukrainian album was shown to Rosenberg and he was asked if he recognized anyone, he singled out Demjanjuk, indicating "that man looks very similar to the Ukrainian Ivan." However, Rosenberg was not willing to identify him with certainty. The man in the photo was older, making identification difficult, because the Ivan he knew was 22 years old at the time. Radiwker explained to Rosenberg that her information indicated that the man he had pointed to (Demjanjuk) was at Sobibor, not Treblinka. Rosenberg insisted that although some of the Ukrainians were known to have been sent to Sobibor, he was certain that he had seen Ivan Demjanjuk up until his last day at Treblinka.

After conferring with a few more survivors, Radiwker was puzzled as to whether Demjanjuk was indeed at Sobibor and not Treblinka. She decided to question some witnesses from Treblinka. Dov Freiberg, shown the photo of Demjanjuk, said it reminded him of someone, but he was not certain just who. Then came Yossef Czarny, who survived Treblinka and ended up at Bergen Belsen. When the photo album of Ukrainian suspects was placed in front of him, Czarny immediately, upon first glance, pointed at Demjanjuk's photo and said, "Ivan Grozny from Treblinka—my God! He lives!" He later told Radiwker that although 33 years had passed, he recognized "Ivan" with full certainty and there could be no mistake. Czarny also insisted that he saw him at Treblinka and that this man could not have been at Sobibor or elsewhere.

That left three more survivors to be interviewed. One of them, a man named Hellman, was unable to identify anyone; when asked if he knew the name Demjanjuk, he replied, "It means nothing to me." However, positive identifications were made by two additional survivors, men named Borak and Lindvasser (the latter served as Treblinka's dentist), and the case being built by Radiwker grew stronger. In addition to the photo identifications in both Israel and the United States, there was the additional evidence contained in the "Trawniki document." This document occupied a central place in the process, during both Demjanjuk's citizenship revocation and extradition and, later, at trial. Trawniki was one of the training camps for Soviet prisoners of war who had volunteered to act as guards (*Wachmanns*) in helping the Germans carry out Operation Reinhardt. The purpose of this operation was to expedite and improve the extermination process by gathering Jews and bringing them to the death camps, where they would be killed in gas chambers. The guards' tasks included guarding the Jews on their way to the gas chambers and conveying them from the trains to various sections of the camps.

A key, but controversial, piece of evidence presented to the court by the prosecution was the Trawniki identification card. Each member of the Trawniki unit was issued an identification card that included personal information and a photo. One such card bore Demjanjuk's photo and indicated his personal information, including place and date of birth. The defense claimed that this card was not originally issued under Demjanjuk's name and, therefore, the card presented to the court was a KGB forgery. After considering the testimony of expert witnesses on behalf of both the prosecution and the defense regarding the authenticity and admissibility of the Trawniki identification card, the court ruled that the card was in fact evidence that the defendant participated in the extermination that took place at Treblinka.

The defendant's alibi concerning the period during which he was alleged to have been at Treblinka was rejected by the court. Demjanjuk contended that in the summer of 1941, during one of the battles between the Germans and the Russian forces, he was wounded and was transferred to four different hospitals until the spring of 1942, when, together with an entire Soviet brigade, he was taken into captivity and held at a POW camp called Chelm. No corroborating evidence was produced by the defense to support this alibi, which was not accepted by the court.

The defense produced several experts who testified that the identification procedures violated several rules of reliable and acceptable identification and were therefore problematic (Wagenaar, 1988). Although no written law exists that requires special training for police officers who conduct lineup or photo identifications, the defense claimed that Radiwker, who was trained as an attorney and employed by the Division for the Investigation of Nazi Crimes (a section of the Israeli Police), was not professionally competent. A cross-examination of Radiwker during the trial illustrated that she did not think it was wrong to direct the witnesses' attention to one specific photo during the identification procedure—a very suggestive method, and one that she acknowledged using. Another problem identified was the fact that all photos presented to witnesses were of possible suspects; no innocent "foils" were included. Under these circumstances, a witness could not make an "error." In addition, the actual report of the identification procedures was inaccurate, as the defense noted. No reference was made in that report (either to U.S. authorities prior to extradition or to the court in Israel) concerning the preparation of the photo lineup, instructions to witnesses, choices made by witnesses during the identification procedure, or information volunteered by those in charge during the identification process. Thus, no report was made concerning negative results (inability to identify anyone). As was made clear during the trial, there were many witnesses (survivors of Treblinka) who did not recognize Demjanjuk as "Ivan the Terrible."

On April 18, 1988, Demjanjuk was convicted in the District Court of Jerusalem of crimes against the Jewish people under Section 1(a)(1) of the Nazi and Nazi Collaborators Law of 1950; crimes against humanity under Section 1(a)(2) of the same law; and war crimes against persecuted people under Section 2(1), together with Section 300 of the Penal Law of 1977. He was sentenced to death. Demjanjuk appealed both the conviction and his death sentence to the Israeli Supreme Court. His appeal commenced on May 14, 1990, more than 2 years after he was found guilty (*Ivan [John] Demjanjuk v. State of Israel,* 1990). A series of events led to the delay of the appeal, the most dramatic of which was the suicide of a member of Demjanjuk's defense team, Dov Eitan, who had previously served as an Israeli district court judge. Eitan, who had joined the defense team only a few months earlier for the appellate process, jumped from the fifteenth floor of a Jerusalem building. The official police investigation produced no satisfactory explanation of his suicide, although one friend reported that Eitan found no solace in the Demjanjuk case.

At Eitan's funeral on December 1, 1988, a 70-year-old man who was a survivor of Treblinka attacked Yoram Sheftel, Demjanjuk's defense attorney, with a solution of hydrochloric acid, shouting, "Eitan's death is because of you." Sheftel was rushed to the hospital and had to undergo several surgical procedures to remove the damaged protective cover of his cornea and transplant a healthy one. The appeal was further delayed by a year to allow Sheftel to recover. The defense was then granted another year to prepare its case. During this delay, many doubts arose concerning the case. New evidence that had not existed during the trial at the lower court was revealed. Much of this evidence became available only after the collapse of the Iron Curtain, which enabled both the defense and the prosecution to conduct more extensive investigations in the former Soviet Union and other Eastern European countries.

The appeal was finally concluded in 1993. Sitting as a Court of Criminal Appeals, in the Supreme Court in Jerusalem, five judges—President Justice Mein Shamgar, Deputy President Justice Menachem Elon, and Justices Aharon Barak, Eliezer Goldberg, and Ya'acov Maltz—courageously reasoned the acquittal of Demjanjuk, based on reasonable doubt, in a verdict that was 400 pages in length. In their analysis of the evidence concerning the appellant's identity, the court found no grounds for interfering with the district court's findings and conclusion. Further, after reviewing the professional literature on eyewitness identification, the court found no reason to believe that lapse of time, in itself, precludes identification. The court also considered additional evidence, consisting of written testimony given in the Soviet Union by *Wachmanns* who were interrogated about their time at Treblinka. Thirty-three of these witnesses named a Ukrainian *Wachmann* called Ivan Marchenko as the person who operated the machines of the gas chambers at the camp and who was, in all probability, the notorious "Ivan the Terrible." This evidence had not been available to the lower court and arose only during the appellate process.

The court then dealt with the interpretation of the concept of "reasonable doubt." Evidence, stated the court, should be consistent, and if there are contradictions, the court is entitled to determine what evidence should be accepted. A reasonable basis should exist for rejecting evidence as untrustworthy. All of the additional evidence in this case consisted of depositions taken in the Soviet Union, without the testimony of those who had taken them. However, the number of depositions created a reasonable doubt that the court could not ignore. After giving this new evidence most serious consideration, the court concluded that it had created a reasonable doubt as to the identity of the appellant as "Ivan the Terrible."

Thus, Demjanjuk was acquitted on the basis of reasonable doubt, demonstrating to Israeli citizens and to the world the importance of justice and reason, especially in trials that occur in such a highly emotional, politicized context and where the defendant (either personally or symbolically) is perceived by many as representing something that is morally repugnant. The five judges, after reaching their final decision in this most controversial case, quite appropriately commented that their decision "was the proper course for judges who cannot examine the heart and mind, but have only what their eyes see and read. The matter is closed but not complete. The complete truth is not the prerogative of the human judge" (*Ivan [John] Demjanjuk v. State of Israel,* 1990).

Note

1. New York State has since streamlined this process and, along with Ohio and a handful of other states, has enacted a special compensation statute for those who are wrongfully imprisoned.

3

How Could This Have Happened?

The Causes and Prevalence of Wrongful Conviction

Quite clearly, there is no accurate, scientific way to determine how many innocent people are convicted, or, put another way, how many of those convicted of crimes are innocent. When we include, as is appropriate, those who plead guilty to crimes they have not committed, the problem becomes more complex, for it is relatively rare for suspects to plead guilty to serious crimes, relatively rare for innocent persons to be given prison terms, and relatively rare for such impropriety and errors to gain the attention of the mass media.

There are, as we write, approximately one million people serving time in U.S. state and federal prisons (not including jails or juvenile facilities), almost all of whom have been convicted of felonies (U.S. Department of Justice, 1995). The number might be slightly reduced by the fact that a few states, such as Delaware, do not have local jails where people are held pending trial; but then it would have to be increased because, in other states, those convicted and sentenced to less than a year often serve their time in local jails. Putting aside the juvenile justice system entirely, where error is even more likely to occur than in the criminal justice process, and putting aside those whose convictions have resulted in suspended sentences or in probation, we are left with about one million adults behind bars. Are there some innocent persons among them? Of that there is no doubt—we will learn that from the newspapers next week, or next month. But how many?

Lacking any figures, those who have written on the subject, or who have given it serious thought, have relied on newspaper accounts that surface, not infrequently but in numbers sufficiently small to make one believe that the prisons are overwhelmingly filled with the guilty; yet not so infrequently that the problem can be disregarded as a tragedy so ominous as to touch the nerve centers and the basic tenets of a criminal justice system.

These newspaper accounts have been collected by several authors, who have usually added other cases gleaned from such sources as interviews with attorneys, court records, interviews with victims of false conviction, and even interviews with victims of crime. Their works almost always consist of a series of anecdotes, with each case a small horror story in itself, yet they provide no data that might give us an estimate of the magnitude of the occurrence, or legal analysis that might show its sources. For one thing, the cases collected are not seriously or sufficiently detailed; often one learns little more than that an innocent person, whose name is given, was arrested for forgery or embezzlement and that after his or her arrest, authorities noted that the events continued to occur, leading them finally to the right culprit and to the exoneration of the wrong one.

In one classic book, Borchard (1932) discusses 60 cases, with an average of only three or four pages devoted to each; other authors have included somewhat fewer cases. Added to these works, of which we have made ample use in our studies (their shortcomings notwithstanding), are extremely interesting book-length accounts of individual cases, the authors of which are convinced that innocent persons have been convicted and either put to death or given lengthy prison terms.

To determine the prevalence of the phenomenon of wrongful conviction, we initially set out to study the perception of its prevalence by criminal justice personnel; it should be noted that the sample of personnel we queried was stacked in favor of obtaining conservative estimates, rather than those who might be more easily persuaded that mistakes are made by "the system." We regard our result, then, as a conservative

TABLE 3.1 Questionnaires Mailed and Returned

Sample	Number Mailed	Number Returned	Percentage Returned
Presiding judges of Ohio county common pleas courts	88	55	63
Ohio county prosecuting attorneys	88	53	60
Ohio county public defenders	28	21	75
Ohio county sheriffs and chiefs of police of 7 major cities	95	59	62
State attorneys general (50 states, American Samoa, Guam, Puerto Rico, District of Columbia)	54	41	76
Totals	353	229	65

SOURCE: Rattner (1983).

prevalence estimation made by a largely conservative sample, most members of which have every reason to defend the system's accuracy and underestimate error. Public defenders, who might be expected to hold a relatively critical view of the system, represented only 9% of respondents.

Concentrating on those closest to the trial process, we asked for respondents' perceptions of the problem both in their own experience and in their own jurisdictions, and as they saw it to exist on a national scale. We mailed 353 questionnaires and received 229 responses (a response rate of approximately 65%). A description of the sample and the responses obtained are shown in Table 3.1.

Before we present any further analysis of the responses, let us turn our attention to the validity and usefulness of perception as a tool for obtaining information of the type we sought, and to the fact that most of the questionnaires mailed and the answers received were from one area of the country, namely, Ohio.

How people perceive a fact, and particularly how they perceive its frequency and prevalence, cannot be a substitute for more objective tests of a quantitative or even a qualitative nature. People may believe that the majority of people in prison are there because they have been convicted of violent crimes, and a study may or may not come up with the same conclusion. Hence, one might well ask, why utilize perception at all, when studies can give us much more accurate results? In one of the few books devoted to this subject, editors Richard L. Henshel and Robert A. Silverman (1975) state in their opening remarks:

> We suggest that a focus upon purposefulness, decision-making, knowledge and ignorance, and perception will be profitable for criminological investigation. This implies not so much a shift in the methods of analysis (although this is often demanded by other advocates of these topics) as a shift in the focal points of whatever methods are used, away from "what *is*" toward "what the relevant actors *think* is." (p. 2-3)

We in no way disagree with this statement—in fact, one of the authors of this volume (Sagarin) contributed an introduction to the Henshel and Silverman volume. We believe, however, that there are specific reasons perception is an important ingredient in the present study.

First, on the issue of wrongful conviction we know of no better way to approach the question of prevalence than through observation. When the actors involved are likely to be the most knowledgeable, to be closest to the situation at hand, we believe that they can come up with data close enough to objective truth to be usable. This does not mean that it is always better to have an approximation than nothing at all: Sometimes the material obtained by asking individuals for their perceptions, or other nonobjective means, can be so misleading as to be worse than having no information whatsoever. It is our conclusion that a survey of the perceptions of the types of persons in our sample concerning the prevalence of false positives offers at least a conservative baseline estimate of how these people see the problem.

Perception has a second usefulness, as pointed out by a long line of prestigious sociologists, from Simmel and Thomas to Merton and Goffman. How people perceive a phenomenon will be one of the determinants of how they act: Perception is a cause of behavior and a key to its understanding. Criminologists have shown that widespread fear of crime—individuals' perception that they are vulnerable—makes a major contribution to behavior on the streets, in our homes, and in our everyday lives. As we shall show in the concluding chapter of this book, if people believe that many innocents are found guilty, this can have a devastating effect on our criminal justice system, and specifically on jury behavior.

In short, perception measures only that; it does not measure the extent or prevalence of a phenomenon. In social science, we have come to rely largely on attitude surveys, and the distinction between an attitudinal study and a perceptual study is weak, but still real. The former, if designed properly, can indicate how the public feels about whether, for example, the criminal justice system is "soft on crime"; but we were attempting to discover not *whether* our sample perceived that many innocents were being imprisoned, important as that turned out to be, but *how frequently* such false imprisonment really takes place. For that reason, the opinions of a random sample, a stratified sample, or some other cross-section of the public at large would not have been of value. Rather, we chose to seek to discover how the problem is perceived by those who are closest to it on a daily basis.

There were others besides those chosen who might have been in our sample—for example, we might have included victims, criminologists, patrol officers on the beat, and prisoners. All of these groups are interesting and worthy of further study, but their inclusion in the survey would have complicated our research, which we limited to those closest to the trial process, not to the crime. Prisoners are a particularly interesting group in this respect. How many people currently in prison insist on their total innocence, or at least of the crimes for which they are serving time? Reaching our ears from the prison walls come wild and often extremely contradictory figures.

Some of the convicted innocents who have come out of prison after several years of unjustified incarceration, emerging completely exonerated, have (in our opinion erroneously but quite understandably) concluded that 25% or even 40% of those behind bars, already convicted, continue to maintain their innocence. Those passing on this information, having been victims themselves, have been ready to believe the inmates from whose company they have only recently departed. Other inmates, of course, boast of their crimes and readily admit their guilt.

This brings us to the question of why we chose to concentrate our efforts in Ohio. One of the reasons for our choice was that all of the authors were either permanently or temporarily located there when this research commenced, and had developed close associations with other criminological researchers, legislators, prison wardens, prosecutors, public defenders, and others in Ohio who were intimately involved in the problem that we were researching. This not only was important in giving us the good return rate we achieved with our questionnaire, it also permitted us to carry out many conversations during the course of this study on the nature of the problem, as these people perceived it.

That was not our only reason, however. Focusing on one state, such as Ohio, serves to control for legal code while still allowing for great diversity of settings. Ohio is the seventh most populous state in the United States, the total number of residents reaching nearly 11 million as of the 1990 U.S. Census. It has an excellent mix of urban, suburban, and rural areas, and a fairly representative criminal justice system. Its racial mixture, inner-city ghettos, and range of ethnicities make it similar to most urban states except that it does not have a large Spanish-speaking population.

Ohio is more typical for our purposes than a southern state, where the question of prejudice and antiblack justice was so rampant during the first half of this century. Ohio is also more representative than a rural state. It shows up in the FBI's *Uniform Crime Reports* with an average rate of felonies (particularly those used for an index of criminality), neither far higher nor lower than that of other states in the area; and its prisons, judged by rate of incarceration per 100,000 population, have commitment rates similar to those of other large states. In fact, the aggregate rate of incarceration for state prisons in the United States in 1993 was 322 per 100,000 population, and Ohio's was 365 per 100,000 (U.S. Department of Justice, 1995, p. 541).

By a coincidence that we could not have foreseen, of about a dozen cases that surfaced with the greatest amount of national and local attention while this study was in progress, two were in Ohio. They were both rape cases, and the rapes had actually occurred, but the wrong men had been arrested and convicted and had been given extraordinarily long prison terms, only to be completely exonerated after some years in prison. This gave us an opportunity to study reactions in the press and among the public; to pick up details as to comments from jurors, witnesses, and prosecutors; and to follow how the released persons were able—or un-able—to get their lives in order. We interviewed attorneys and others personally involved, and were able to scrutinize carefully the progress of the process, from suspicion that there had been a serious error through exoneration and postexoneration.

We know of no previous study that has attempted to quantify the phenomenon of wrongful conviction, but we were able to clarify the issue to some degree by examining the work of Kalven and Zeisel (1966), who conducted one of the classic studies of the American jury. In drawing upon this work, we had to do some speculating, but Kalven and Zeisel's data, when extrapolated, brought us to approximately the same conclusion as that we drew from our survey of the perceptions of criminal justice personnel, as we will demonstrate.

In their study of criminal cases, Kalven and Zeisel obtained the cooperation of a large number of judges. Each judge, after giving the charge to the jury, would then write down the decision that he would render had there been a trial without a jury (as most criminal trials actually are today, in the United States). The judge was not to predict what he expected the jury to do; he was only to write down what he himself would do in rendering a decision, now that the trial, except for the jury verdict, was completed. In about 19% of all cases studied, the judge and jury disagreed. In these cases of disagreement, the jury voted not guilty in 15% of the cases, in which the judge would have found the accused guilty. In the other 4%, the reverse was the case.

Our study focuses on the falsely convicted (false positives), not on those improperly freed (the false negatives), and hence we can ignore for the moment the 15% who were found not guilty against the predisposition of the judge. More relevant to our study is the fact that in fully 4% of all cases in which the judge believed that a verdict of guilt was unwarranted, that verdict was nonetheless rendered by the jury, despite the safeguards of our system. It is possible that some of these people were in fact guilty and the jury was exercising more wisdom than the judge; it is likewise possible that the judge might not have considered the accused innocent, but only that guilt was not established beyond a reasonable doubt, or that his finding of not guilty would have been based on technical reasons, rather than on belief in innocence. Nonetheless, when all these factors are considered, we are left with a slightly eroded 4% of people who, in the opinions of judges, were not guilty yet were found guilty by juries.

A judge will sometimes set aside a verdict of this type as being against the weight of the evidence, but this is rare; judges are legally permitted to do so, but the jury is legally considered to be the trier of fact, and judges are reluctant to overrule juries on precisely this point: the facts of the case. In the rare instance when a judge sets aside a verdict, the action is appealable by the prosecution, and if the verdict is not reinstated, the accused may be tried again, without such a trial constituting double jeopardy.

Now, let us speculate from the 4% discrepancy figure. Assume that in half of these cases, the jury was right and the judge wrong—an assumption that is conservative, for juries are much more likely than judges to be swayed by irrelevancies, by material stricken from the record but that they have heard and been told to disregard, and by sentimentality that may favor the accused. This leaves us with innocent persons being found guilty in 2% of all cases. Now, let us assume that in half of *these* cases, the guilty verdict is successfully appealed. This, too, is a conservative estimate, because appeals are much more likely in major cases than in minor ones, and some of these may have been automobile thefts, rather than armed robbery, forcible rape, or murder; further, not all appeals are successful.

Judges in such cases are unlikely to have made procedural decisions during the course of these trials that have been prejudicial to the defendants; the fact that at some time during the trials the judges had begun to come to the conclusion that the accused were innocent would have militated against such rulings. If it is a question of the weight of the evidence, here, too, appeals courts have the legal right to overturn guilty verdicts on these grounds, but are reluctant to do so; like judges, appellate courts tend to defer to juries as the triers of fact. But, despite these obstacles, if one-half of the cases are successfully appealed, and if in all such successful appeals either the prosecution does not proceed with new trials or the defendants are found not guilty in new trials, this still leaves 1% of all convictions as erroneously decided against innocent people.

To balance this, note that not all of the 1% would go to prison. When a judge is convinced that a defendant is innocent, there is a greater likelihood of a suspended sentence or of probation, although there are limits to judges' discretion in this regard, particularly, as is so often the case with convicted innocents, if the defendant has a previous criminal record, even if it is unrelated to the crime of which the person has recently been falsely convicted. Balancing this is still another factor that would tend to inflate the 1% figure, namely, the large number of people who plead guilty, mainly on minor offenses (other than traffic laws), who are innocent but wish to get an unfortunate situation over and done with.

Now, let us look at how our own sample of judges, prosecutors, public defenders, and others saw this situation. In our questionnaire, we made

TABLE 3.2 Estimates of Wrongful Conviction in the United States

Category	f	% (relative)	% (adjusted)
Never	10	4.4	5.6
Less than 1%	127	55.5	71.8
1–5%	36	15.7	20.3
6–10%	4	1.7	2.3
Missing	52	22.7	—
Totals	N = 229	100.0	100.0

no effort to raise the problem of innocent suspects making guilty pleas, and it is not at all certain whether or not the respondents took this issue into account in making their estimates of the pervasiveness of false conviction, as they perceive it. The estimates we received ranged from zero (an unbelievable figure, in light of what was on the front pages of Ohio newspapers at the time) up to 5% of all cases, with most responses hovering near the 1% mark. Table 3.2 summarizes the estimates of our conservative sample.[1] With these figures before us, and side by side with the experience of Kalven and Zeisel (1966), we decided to see what the magnitude of the problem would appear to be if we cut the 1% figure in half, on the grounds that most of our respondents selected the category "less than 1%," thereby indicating that they believed wrongful conviction does occur (they rejected "never"), but also indicating that it occurs in less than 1% of all felony convictions. Given that the midpoint between zero and 1% is 0.5%, we felt justified in using that figure.

We are left with what appears to be an impressive figure for accuracy and justice: 99.5% of all guilty verdicts in felony cases are handed down on people who did indeed commit the crimes of which they have been accused. But in terms of real numbers, this figure is more disheartening. According to the U.S. Department of Justice's Bureau of Justice Statistics (1995, p. 374), the estimated total number of persons arrested and charged with index crimes in 1993 was 2,848,400.[2] Conviction rates vary from state to state and by type of offense, but based on the best available data, an analysis of the likelihood of felony conviction in the nation's 75 largest counties, we can reasonably assume that about 70% of all felony arrests result in conviction (U.S. Department of Justice, 1995, p. 497). Now, if we go to our survey data and to the study of the American jury, and assume that 70% of those arrested for index crimes are convicted, this would yield the following estimate of wrongful conviction for the eight crimes in the FBI index only:

1990 arrests for index crimes	2,848,400
× conviction rate (70%)	×0.7
1990 convictions for index crimes	1,993,880
× wrongful conviction rate (0.5%)	×.005
Estimated number of wrongful convictions	9,969

Thus, if these apparently conservative estimates are reasonable, we are facing an interesting dilemma: A high volume of prosecutions, even if 99.5% accurate when guilty verdicts are rendered, can still generate about 10,000 erroneous convictions for index crimes in a single year. And this figure does not including the many erroneous convictions that occur in cases involving crimes not in the index; when these are added to the 10,000 "index false positives," the result is even more sobering.

In order to come to some conclusion regarding the sources of these errors, we studied previous works on the conviction of the innocent, limiting ourselves to American cases that have occurred since 1900. International cases are not represented in our database, but we utilize some in the discussions that follow to illustrate the cross-cultural nature of this type of injustice. Further, we did not include the many cases in which there are serious and reasonable doubts as to the guilt of the accused—we were concerned only with those in which innocence has been clearly established. We did not include any cases in which people were held for lengthy periods and then acquitted or released, despite their suffering and injustice, because our emphasis is on the wrongful *conviction* process.

We created an initial database of 205 cases from the following sources:

- Edward D. Radin (1964), 60 cases
- Edwin Borchard (1932), 54 cases
- Newspaper clippings, legal documents, and miscellaneous sources (recent), 42 cases
- Jerome Frank and Barbara Frank (1957), 29 cases

- Erle Stanley Gardner (1952), 13 cases
- Sarah Ehrmann (1962), 5 cases
- Elizabeth Loftus (1979), 2 cases

There is no doubt that the cases to some extent reflect the diverse occupational range of those who collected, studied, and published information on them. Jerome Frank was a noted jurist, a trusted adviser to Franklin D. Roosevelt, and a judge of the U.S. Circuit Court of Appeals; Elizabeth Loftus is a psychologist specializing in eyewitness identification; Erle Stanley Gardner, an attorney and professor of law, won renown both for his detective fiction and for his efforts on behalf of innocents who were convicted; Sarah Ehrmann was active for half a century in the American League to Abolish Capital Punishment.

Probably the least publicized cases are those in which the wrongfully convicted person received some penal sanction less severe than imprisonment. Clearly, felony offenses are overrepresented among the cases publicized as false positives, and the more serious the offense, the more likely it is to come to public attention—find its way into newspapers and books, and in other ways come to light. Or, one might say, the more serious the offense and the greater the sentence (often capital punishment or several life imprisonment terms to be run consecutively, or first eligibility for parole when the individual has reached an advanced age), the more likely there will be continued investigation, appeals, and struggles, until the day of exoneration arrives. No one would have heard of Dreyfus had he simply been given a dishonorable discharge from the French army, or of the Scottsboro boys if they had been beaten up, given 6-month prison terms, and sent back to their freight trains.

Of the cases in our initial database, 45% involved murder or manslaughter; about 30.5% involved robbery, particularly armed robbery; and about 12.5% involved rape. However, when a distinction is drawn between older cases (those occurring between 1900 and 1960) and those since 1961, the wrongful convictions on forcible rape go up, reaching 35.7% of all cases in recent years. Whether this is a result of increased community pressure to make arrests and obtain convictions in rape cases or of increased interest in rape, along with longer sentences and greater willingness to bring such offenses to public attention, we are not certain.

Why do such cases occur? What are the sources of these errors in the criminal justice system? Table 3.3 shows the distribution of the types of

TABLE 3.3 Distribution of Types of Errors Contributing to Wrongful
Conviction

Type of Error	f	% (relative)	% (adjusted)
Eyewitness misidentification	100	48.8	52.3
Perjury by witness	21	10.2	11.0
Negligence by criminal justice officials	19	9.3	9.9
Pure error (2)	16	7.8	8.4
Coerced confession	16	7.8	8.4
"Frame up" (3)	8	3.9	4.2
Perjury by criminal justice officials	5	2.4	2.6
Identification by police due to prior criminal record	3	1.5	1.6
Forensic errors (4)	3	1.5	1.6
Other errors (missing data)	14	6.8	—
Totals	N = 205	100.0	100.0

errors that make major contributions to such injustices, based upon an
analysis of all cases in our database, with only the major single source of
error for each case identified. The issue is far more complex than the table
indicates, however, for there is almost always more than one force at work.
If we had to isolate a single "system dynamic" that pervades large numbers
of these cases, we would probably describe it as *police and prosecutorial
overzealousness:* the anxiety to solve a case; the ease with which one
having such anxiety is willing to believe, on the slightest evidence of the
most negligible nature, that the culprit is in hand; the willingness to use
improper, unethical, and illegal means to obtain a conviction when one
believes that the person at the bar is guilty.

Thus, although the database tells us something about the causes of the
false convictions in all but 14 instances, it is insufficient. Eyewitness
misidentifications are typically made in good faith, but the heading itself
tells us nothing about the conditions under which such identifications

have been made, whether police have shown a witness a picture of a suspect before the lineup, whether the identifying witness was unsure and was urged to be more positive when testifying in court. All we know is that, in slightly more than half of the cases in which one major cause could be found, that cause was eyewitness misidentification.

Furthermore, we do not know whether these misidentifications were made by persons of the same races as the convicted innocents or other races, or, if the witnesses' races differed from those of the suspects, whether prejudice and unfamiliarity played a part. Nor do we know anything about the conditions of light and dark when the crimes were committed, or about the distance and duration of interaction between witnesses and perpetrators, or about previous contact between the wrongfully accused and the mistaken witnesses. We discuss all of these factors extensively in Chapter 4.

Drawing from both the analysis of the database in Table 3.3 and the extensive analysis of more recent cases, from which we were able to glean a great deal of information, we discovered that it was increasingly obvious that several factors were often simultaneously at work. In fact, these "interaction effects" are so important that isolating any one individual factor misses the point—we typically see, in these cases, system failure, with more than one error occurring.

Furthermore, although we have since had an opportunity to review reports of several hundred more recent cases reported in the mass media and in scholarly publications, this review has not produced any new factors that were not present in our original database. The patterns are distressingly similar, with eyewitness error, police and prosecutorial overzealousness, and perjury interacting to produce system failure. Moreover, these elements interact in such complex ways that any simple tabular listing of cases by "types of errors" would be a gross oversimplification and would be misleading. We have decided not to present such a table (beyond the original 205 cases that led us to our key factors), because our sources typically lack the detailed case-level information necessary to understand these interaction effects.

In subsequent chapters, we shall discuss both eyewitness identification and false confessions, particularly those obtained without brutality and after *Miranda* warnings have been given. The following is a brief summary, based on both the database analysis (Table 3.3) and detailed studies of individual cases, most of the latter since 1960, of the major causes of error resulting in wrongful conviction. We have discussed a number of these recent cases in Chapter 2, along with more historically prominent exemplars of false positives.

How Does It Happen?

How can an innocent defendant be convicted? What would possibly induce an innocent person to plead guilty? What goes wrong with a criminal justice system that has created an elaborate system of safeguards to protect the rights of suspects and defendants—a system that gave us *Powell* (1932), *Mapp* (1961), *Gideon* (1963), and *Miranda* (1966), among many others?

By interviewing convicted innocents, attorneys, and other key informants, and by analyzing hundreds of individual cases, mostly of relatively recent vintage, we were able to add considerably to the cases that made up our original database. Despite assessing more than 500 acknowledged false positives (with more called to our attention each month), we remain convinced that in these cases, police and prosecutorial overzealousness and eyewitness error (usually unintentional), along with perjury, are pervasive, and that the most likely scenario is one in which these factors interact to produce system failure, resulting in the conviction of an innocent person.

Eyewitness Error

We believe that the single most important factor leading to wrongful conviction in the United States and England (Brandon & Davies, 1973) is eyewitness misidentification, to which we could add, in good faith. This is shown not only in our database, but in the responses to our questionnaire, where nearly 8 out of 10 ranked witness error (primarily witness misidentification, but also including some less frequent types of witness error) as by far the most frequent type of error leading to false conviction. This is shown in Table 3.4 and discussed in detail in a later chapter. Other studies have also emphasized the importance of eyewitness error (but see Bedau & Radelet, 1987, p. 61; Radelet & Bedau, 1992).

TABLE 3.4 Estimates (Rank Order) of Types of Errors Leading to Wrongful Conviction

Rank Order	Judicial Error		Police Error		Witness Error		Prosecutorial Error	
	f	%	f	%	f	%	f	%
1	6	3.8	22	13.9	125	78.6	5	3.2
2	10	6.4	107	67.6	17	10.7	22	14.1
3	32	20.5	11	7.0	11	6.9	100	64.1
4	108	69.2	18	11.4	6	3.8	29	18.6
	mean = 3.55		mean = 2.1		mean = 1.34		mean = 2.9	

NOTE: Errors were ranked on a scale that ranged from 1 = *most frequent* to 4 = *least frequent*.

Intermingled with eyewitness error is the question of rewards. Is a person likely to be more positive, on the witness stand, that a given defendant is the person he or she saw if the witness has either a financial incentive (reward) or plea-bargaining/sentencing incentive? A number of jurisdictions have begun to scrutinize the use of informants, especially jailhouse "snitches" and narcotics informants, because such testimony has often been linked with wrongful conviction.

Race plays an important role in eyewitness identification, and this is probably as true of relatively unprejudiced witnesses as it is of more prejudiced witnesses. It is difficult to look at the Lenell Geter case without seeing the specter of race, not only because of the meager evidence of eyewitnesses whose testimony alone resulted in this false conviction, but also because the judge demonstrated such prejudice when he sentenced this educated, employed, first-time "offender," on a robbery charge, to life imprisonment.

In 1967, the U.S. Supreme Court handed down decisions in three landmark cases involving eyewitness identification, in which the Court sought to establish effective constitutional safeguards and guidelines governing the admission of such evidence in federal and state criminal trials. In *United States v. Wade* (1967), the Court decided that the postindictment lineup (or police parade, as it is known in England) is a critical stage at which an accused is entitled to the aid of counsel. The Court noted the great possibility of unfairness in a lineup at which counsel is not present. In the *Wade* case, bank employees who had witnessed the robbery of their bank were allowed to see the accused in the custody of the FBI before the lineup began.

On the same day the *Wade* decision was handed down, the Court also decided *Gilbert v. California* (1967), a case involving the murder of a police officer during an armed robbery. Again, there was a lineup, this time 16 days after the appointment of counsel, who was not notified. In-court identifications were made by witnesses who were present at the lineup, and the Court determined that the accused had been deprived of the right to counsel.

In the last case of the trilogy handed down that day, *Stovall v. Denno* (1967), a murder suspect had been taken to the hospital bedside of the slain man's widow for her to make an identification. The widow identified him as the killer, and the accused was convicted. The Court upheld the legality of this identification, ruling that there was no denial of due process, because the widow was the only person who could exonerate the suspect, she could not go to the police station for the usual lineup, and there was no way of knowing how long she might live. This was a decision that elicited strong dissent. It would appear that it might have been more appropriate to bring several possible suspects, or the equivalent of a lineup, to the widow's bedside, so that she could have chosen from among them; whether this would have been more stressful to the ailing and grieving woman, and whether such stress must take precedence over the rights of a defendant or an accused, would be arguable.

Although jurors attach great significance to eyewitness testimony, experts and judges increasingly share the view of Judge Lumbard of the Second Circuit, who has observed:

> Centuries of experience in the administration of criminal justice have shown that convictions based solely on testimony that identifies a defendant previously unknown to the witness is highly suspect. Of the various kinds of evidence it is the least reliable, especially where unsupported by corroborating evidence. (*Jackson v. Fogg,* 1978)

Despite the steps taken by the Supreme Court to establish safeguards against eyewitness misidentification, such errors continue to surface. In 1982, a Texas prisoner, Howard Mosley of Galveston, who had been convicted in a stabbing death and sentenced to a life term, was exonerated after new evidence indicated that the crime had been committed by a man who also admitted killing 10 others ("Monday Finally Comes," 1982). In a highly publicized Ohio case where great weight was placed on eyewitness identification by the victims of rape, William Jackson spent nearly 5 years in prison for rapes that he did not commit. He was released from prison after a grand jury indicted another Ohio man (also named Jackson, but unrelated) on 36 counts of rape and 46 counts of aggravated burglary ("Freed Jackson's Advice," 1982; "Ohio Doctor Accused," 1982).

In the Jackson case, both the innocent and the guilty defendants were black, and the innocent one had been identified by several white eyewitnesses, an indication of the special difficulties in interracial identification. Nonetheless, there were some similarities in resemblance: The two Jacksons were of approximately the same height, both wore Afro hairstyles, and their facial shapes and mustaches were similar as well. By contrast, in the Texas case, Mosley was fully a foot taller than Watts, the actual offender, but was misidentified by witnesses to the point where the jury did not have a reasonable doubt.

Accounts of eyewitness error are myriad, and sometimes bizarre. In one incredible case, Jeffrey Streeter was convicted without even having been arrested. Streeter had been sitting outside a courtroom and was asked by a defense attorney if he would sit next to him as a way of testing the credibility of the eyewitnesses. The defense attorney failed to inform the judge of the switch. Despite the fact that the actual defendant was also in the courtroom at the time, three eyewitnesses unflinchingly pointed to the startled Streeter, seated next to the defense attorney, as the criminal. Streeter was convicted and sentenced to a year in jail for assaulting an elderly man. However, he spent only one night in jail before being released on his own recognizance, and his conviction was subsequently reversed ("Court Stand-in Is Convicted," 1980).

In another case, Robert Duncan, president of the Missouri Association of Criminal Defense Lawyers, was representing a Mexican American defendant who had been arrested after being identified by a woman who was raped by "an Italian-looking man." When a second suspect was brought in, she identified him, too, as the same guilty offender. She reportedly told authorities, "I'm getting tired of coming down here to identify this man." According to the defense attorney, "The second guy didn't look anything at all like my client" ("When Nightmare of False Arrest," 1984, p. 46).

Prosecutorial and
Police Misconduct and Errors

Far too many cases come from the states to the Supreme Court presenting dismal pictures of official lawlessness, of illegal searches and seizures, illegal detentions attended by prolonged interrogation and coerced admissions of guilt, of the denial of counsel, and downright brutality.
                    William J. Brennan, *The Bill of Rights and the States,* 1961

Some of the improprieties committed by police and prosecutors are directed against guilty people, but this makes them no more legal or proper; many of the most famous landmark cases brought before the Supreme Court concerning such improprieties have resulted in the freeing of blatantly culpable individuals. This was true of Miranda and Escobedo, for example, but not of Ozzie Powell and the other Scottsboro defendants, or of Bradley Cox in Ohio. The reasons for police and prosecutorial misconduct should be distinguished from the types of misconduct that occur. The reason generally given for such misconduct is the firm belief that the person in custody, or under suspicion, is guilty, and it is therefore a public service to get him or her into the slammer, or even executed, even if that might involve bending the rules, flexing authoritarian muscles, suppressing some evidence, or other acts of wrongdoing.

Overzealousness is a term often applied to this type of investigation and prosecution, and although we do not dispute that such a factor can exist, it is not simple. Overzealousness itself might not arise from so noble a motive as generally stated; it might come from a desire to add points to a scorecard, to enhance a reputation as a tough and successful prosecutor because of an impending election, or to receive commendation and promotion in the police department for having nabbed a vicious criminal and solved a difficult case. Overzealousness might also conceal bigotry and racism, or sometimes greed. In England, a chief detective secretly divided the reward money that was given to the major prosecution witness in one of the cases described by Ludovic Kennedy. The detective himself went to prison eventually, although the men he had helped to convict were not freed; they even met on one occasion in a prison yard.

Largely overlooked in previous discussions of overzealousness has been the possibility that it may sometimes derive from the inability, unwillingness, or lack of funds and personnel available to police to make true and proper investigations. It is clearly easier to close a case where there is grave doubt about the suspect's guilt than to continue to pursue it until there is sufficient reason to be confident the accused is guilty and to gather enough legally acceptable evidence to prove that in court. Caseload pressure, the need to close cases and move on to others, is powerful, and many law enforcement officials have privately (and sometimes publicly) acknowledged this problem.

Police and prosecutorial improprieties take on several different forms: coaching witnesses at lineups but denying such coaching under oath; obtaining confessions through brutality, threat, force, or guile, and denying any such actions in court; planting evidence, such as a gun or drugs, that will militate against the accused; making threats against potential witnesses for the accused; using rewards and offers of immunity to entice those willing to testify; and suppressing exculpatory evidence even after motions for discovery have been made.

Item: A prosecutor brings as evidence a pair of men's undershorts found a mile from the crime scene. Alleging that these shorts belong to the accused and are heavily stained with blood that is the same type as the victim's, the prosecutor calls a chemist, who verifies this incriminating information. The defense requests, and is denied, an opportunity to examine the shorts (a judicial error that will subsequently be corrected by a higher court). Despite the defendant's denial that the shorts—the only link in a chain of rather meager evidence—are his, the jury brings in a verdict of guilty. The convicted prisoner subsequently petitions the Supreme Court for a writ of habeas corpus. The shorts are produced, by order of the Court, and a microanalyst appears for the petitioner and testifies that they are stained not with blood, but with red paint. The prosecutor later admits having known that the stains were paint—a fact not only unrevealed to the jury and defense, but deliberately misrepresented in a manner that comes perilously close to subornation of perjury by the prosecutor (*Miller v. Pate,* 1967).

Item: Two men are arrested and convicted of armed robbery and first-degree murder, and are sentenced to life imprisonment without eligibility for parole. Sullivan admits his part in the crime, but claims that Reissfelder was not his partner. After spending 16 years in prison, never wavering in his protestation of innocence, Reissfelder is exonerated. Five policemen, an FBI agent, and a probation officer submit statements indicating that the authorities conducting the original investigation knew at the time of the trial and conviction that Reissfelder was not a party to the crime ("16 Years in Jail," 1983). The law is clear—the defense is entitled to have any evidence that might prove exculpatory—but in this case, again, prosecutors knew they had the wrong man and yet were intent on continuing the prosecution. Although the prosecutor's job is to seek justice, and not just convictions, in some cases winning the conviction clearly takes precedence.

A duplicate of the above case occurred in California, where two defendants were convicted of murdering a 65-year-old man. One confessed to the murder, but the other, Juan Venegas, spent 2½ years in prison following conviction, protesting his innocence. When finally released and exonerated, he mounted a civil suit against the state and was awarded $1 million (an award that was later reduced substantially). Evidence at the civil trial showed that the police intimidated witnesses to perjure them-selves and to orchestrate a frame-up of Venegas (Granelli, 1980; "Innocent Prisoner," 1980).

Plea Bargaining

Many innocent defendants are convicted after entering guilty pleas. For most people, these may be the most puzzling of all cases of convicted innocents (for guilty pleas must be counted as convictions). After all, why would a perfectly innocent person plead guilty? This is one of the least publicized dynamics of wrongful conviction. One of the reasons for the lack of publicity is that most—although not all—of these "bargains" result in immediate freedom, suspended sentences, or perhaps probation, and hence in these cases there is no continued aftermath, no investigation, no exoneration. The revocation of a guilty plea is legally permitted only under limited conditions; for example, when a judge refuses to abide by a bargain that has been made between the defendant, through counsel, and the prosecution. Ordinarily, a plea bargain closes the case.

There are ample reasons some innocent persons plead guilty. In a social psychological experiment utilizing role playing, Gregory, Mowen, and Linder (1978) found that innocent persons, playing the role of defendants, were more likely to accept plea bargains when they faced a number of charges or when the probable severity of punishment, as they perceived and feared it, was great. Such experiments are particularly relevant in an era when executions have been resumed in the United States and are frequent in certain states, such as Florida and Texas. When their lives are at stake, innocent persons who have been wrongly identified or who have been victims of perjury and forged documentation that their defense attorneys are unable to combat are greatly tempted to make deals. Even though they might be facing long prison terms, they live with the hope that eventually the truth will be discovered and they will be freed.

Such was the situation in Richmond, Virginia, when Harry Siegler, who maintained his innocence throughout his trial, sat and watched an alarm-ingly strong case being made against him. Siegler was charged with first-degree murder, and, as Virginia is among the states that have capital punishment laws that have been upheld as constitutional by the U.S. Supreme Court, he feared the jury would find him guilty and sentence him to death by electrocution. While awaiting the jury's verdict, the defendant, in desperation, changed his plea to guilty in a bargain that would result in a term of life imprisonment. A few minutes later, the jury came in with its verdict: not guilty. We cite this case not because we are certain of Siegler's innocence (we are not), but because it illustrates the potential importance of severe punishments, such as execution, in inducing defendants, some of whom may be innocent, to plead guilty (but see Bedau & Radelet, 1987, p. 63).

In cases involving less serious charges, a defendant who is unable to make bail and is offered, in exchange for a plea of guilty, immediate release with nothing more consequential than a minor criminal record (a typical scenario in communities where such records are not uncommon and not highly stigmatizing) cannot easily resist the lure of a guilty plea. Even if the defendant knows him- or herself to be guiltless, a finding of not guilty is not at all certain if a case goes to trial.

For those caught up in the criminal justice system, and whose incomes do not qualify them for assistance from public defenders or legal aid organizations, legal fees are extraordinarily high. If a person is charged with disorderly conduct, simple assault, or resisting arrest (the completely innocent, in their outrage, often do resist arrest), he or she may be most eager to have the episode over with, and to walk out of court with a guilty plea, rather than return for many more court appearances and pay additional funds to an attorney. Those who believe that, having established their innocence, they will be able to turn around and file civil suits for costs and compensation for pain and humiliation are, with few exceptions, indulging in pipe dreams.

A guilty plea is usually accompanied by a ritualistic colloquy between the judge and the accused, in which the judge may subtly compel the defendant to confess to his or her guilt. Insofar as there has been a bargain, the judge does not wish to clutter the record with the suspicion that an innocent person has been compelled to plead guilty. There is an interesting point of distinction that is often overlooked: A plea of not guilty is not considered a denial of guilt, but rather a prayer to the court that one be found not guilty, and an expression that one chooses to go to trial to emerge with such a finding; a plea of guilty, on the other hand, is almost always thought of as a confession of guilt. That it might be entered into for reasons other than a defendant's culpability is given scant attention.

Community Pressure for Conviction

The action of the Israeli Supreme Court in the Demjanjuk case, described in Chapter 2, was both principled and courageous in the face of extensive public pressure to convict "Ivan the Terrible." However, in periods of high crime rates and great public outcry against criminals, and when group pressures are felt in the courtroom, conviction rates may be higher than at other times. Groups united by some common bond are, in fact, often referred to as pressure groups, and it is undeniable that efforts to influence what is happening in the world often extend to the courtroom. Groups that have sought to have such influence include ethnic and racial groups, women's groups, and homosexual and antihomosexual groups, as well as others. In the famous rape case in New Bedford, Massachusetts, in which both the victim and the defendants were of Portuguese descent, the Portuguese American community attempted to exert pressure before, during, and after the trial, while feminist groups and their allies were fighting with equal vigor on the other side. It is possible that the increase in the number of instances of false imprisonment in rape cases that have come to light since the early 1970s may be due in part to increased pressure to obtain convictions in rape cases; by contrast, the majority of rape charges in the earlier part of the century were almost invariably directed against blacks, and were a manifestation of racist community pressure.

When community and group pressure and prejudice against an accused individual are high, the situation is sometimes handled by a call for a change of venue. The court must allow a change of venue at defense request if mob violence threatens (*Blevins v. State,* 1963) or it if appears or proves to be impossible to select an impartial jury in the original venue (*People v. Harris,* 1981). The court must consider all relevant factors, including the scope and source of publicity, the nature and gravity of the offense, the size of the community and the defendant's status therein, the popularity and prominence of the victims, inconvenience to the prosecution and to the administration of justice if the venue is changed, and the likelihood of finding a substantially better or fairer jury panel elsewhere (*State v. Engel,* 1980). Even when changes of venue are granted, the results are not always trials that are free from pressures; witness the Scottsboro case, where the change of venue from Scottsboro to Decatur, another small, rural Alabama town with an equal amount of prejudice in the 1930s, proved fruitless in diminishing community pressure to convict the innocent.

Pressure from the public, sometimes intensified by news media coverage, as in the Sheppard case, can be an expression of democratic participation in the criminal justice process. It can sometimes make the system more responsive to the social needs, values, and feelings of large numbers of citizens. It can serve as a watchdog, lest corruption and malfeasance in the system go unnoticed or the rich and powerful who deserve some form of punishment remain unindicted. Such a spotlight on the courts may thus result in the prosecution of cases that warrant pursuit, but that might otherwise be dropped because of the standing and influence of accused perpetrators and their families, or in appropriate findings of not guilty. It is difficult to believe that Joanne Little or Angela Davis would have been found anything other than guilty had it not been for public pressure. When members of the Black Panthers and other militants were arrested, the president of Yale University startled the country by stating that he doubted if a black person could receive a fair trial in America, a statement that probably acted as a self-fulfilling prophecy. Likewise, absent national and even international pressure, how many arrests and successful prosecutions would have occurred in the case of the three civil rights workers who were murdered in Mississippi in 1964?

Public pressure, then, is a two-edged sword. In some cases it may force courts to deal more fairly with certain suspects than they otherwise might have, but it may also simply reflect the public's fears and desires for vengeance, feelings that are easily manipulated by demagogues who are ready and willing to oblige.

Inadequacy of Counsel

The right to counsel is now well established in the United States. Despite the Bill of Rights, which sets out this right quite clearly, it took several cases to establish it in some states; important in this regard are the cases of *Powell v. Alabama* (1932), *Gideon v. Wainwright* (1963), and *Argersinger v. Hamlin* (1972). In the conviction of the innocent, an important factor is not the right to counsel, but the counsel's adequacy. In fact, that was the issue in the case of Ozzie Powell, one of the Scottsboro boys, who was represented, in a halfhearted and blatantly incompetent manner, by counsel barely interested in Powell's case, much less his welfare. It was only because this was a capital case that the Supreme Court ruled that Powell had been deprived of due process of law, as guaranteed by the Fourteenth Amendment.

That some people are convicted because their lawyers have little experience, caseloads that are too large, and inadequate budgets to carry out excellent investigations is evident. Counsel for Bradley Cox (falsely convicted of rapes actually committed by Jon Simonis, "the ski mask rapist") worked hard, but he was a harried public defender who gave Cox permission to take a polygraph test without counsel present, who missed at least one major opportunity for a mistrial, and whose cross-examination of the detectives who had obtained the false confession was anything but hard-hitting. We examine the dynamics of Cox's case in detail in Chapter 5, in the context of false confessions.

Few cases are overturned on the basis of inadequacy or incompetence of counsel; exoneration seldom comes because of such an appeal being upheld, but because of other developments. The rationale that the original defense counsel, for whatever reasons, did not adequately represent the client's interests in the case makes the appeal difficult to win. Collegial relationships within the legal profession, though pitting lawyer against lawyer as adversaries, generally stop short of promoting the idea of attacking colleagues for mishandling cases, just as doctors are not eager to testify against other doctors, police against police, and so forth. Lawyers assigned anew, or on appeal, are not eager to pursue this line to gain reversals, preferring to characterize as "new" evidence anything that was previously overlooked.

Errors that defense attorneys may make include failing to make discovery motions and to pursue them vigorously; using poor judgment in deciding whether or not to put a defendant on the stand; allowing a defendant to take a polygraph test, especially in the absence of the defense counsel; and failing to challenge vigorously the contentions made by the prosecution in court (Finer, 1973).

Accusations Against
the Innocent by the Guilty

Item: Nathaniel Carter is arrested for murder in the stabbing death of Clarice Herndon. Carter's chief accuser is his estranged wife, who testifies that she watched helplessly as Carter attacked her foster mother with a knife, inflicting 23 stab wounds. Carter is sentenced to a prison term of 25 years to life, his flawless record notwithstanding, on the basis of the accusation of one self-stated eyewitness weighted against his own denial and verifiable alibi. After he has served 2 years in prison, his ex-wife, under complete immunity, admits that she, in fact, was the one who killed her foster mother. The police explain that the cuts on Mrs. Carter's hands at the time of the crime led them to believe that she, too, had been attacked by her former husband. If she seemed to be the perfect witness, the police were far from perfect investigators ("How Errors Convicted," 1984), as we have discussed in Chapter 2.

In the two cases explored by Ludovic Kennedy in his books about miscarriages of justice in Great Britain, the killer was the chief witness against the innocent accused, and each case rested almost entirely on the actual murderer's perjured testimony. Such was true of Timothy Evans, whose hanging for the murders committed by his accuser, Christie, is described in *Ten Rillington Place* (Kennedy, 1961/1985b). In a case in which three men were convicted (one later to be freed because of the impregnability of his alibi) for the murder of a postmaster, the man who pointed the finger at the three innocent people was himself the murderer (he also collected a part of the reward for helping to solve the crime). When it became known that the convictions were based almost solely on the accusation of the actual murderer, one judge found this nearly impossible to believe, saying that to allow innocent people to go to prison for long terms because of what one has oneself committed is to be "wicked beyond belief" (a phrase used as the title of one of Kennedy's books). Such a statement from a judge who had been handling criminal cases for many years is, we believe, an indication of naïveté beyond belief.

There is yet another type of false accusation, in which the chief witness against the accused is not the one who committed the crime, but one who falsely claims victimization in a crime that never took place. An example is the accuser of Robert Daniels, who was a student who lived in a coed dormitory. While he was talking to a female student in the dorm hallway, a door to one of the rooms off the hall opened and the room's occupant asked Daniels and the woman to speak more quietly. The woman he was speaking to then invited Daniels into her room, where they continued their conversation and later went to bed together. A few hours afterward, Daniels got up and dressed, went to his own room for a little more sleep, then spent the day attending classes, as did the woman with whom he had passed a few hours the evening before. Her day was different from his in one respect, however: At the end of her school day, she went to the police and reported that she had been raped. That evening, Daniels was arrested. The alleged victim's word was the only evidence against Daniels's denial, but weighing against him was that he had a criminal past and the woman appeared to be the epitome of everything righteous and proper. Daniels was convicted and sent to prison. His innocence did not come to light until the complaining witness in his case was arrested for arson and claimed that she was committing such acts because of the trauma of the rape. A suspicious prosecutor delved deeper into the woman's life and found that she had a history of mental illness and was under a therapist's care. The therapist later admitted that he knew of the false charge of rape and of Daniels's imprisonment, but claimed that he could say nothing because of the confidentiality of the doctor-patient relationship.

Accusations regarding crimes that never occurred are not limited to rape, child molestation, and other sex cases. There have been several cases in which men have served prison terms for murders that never took place; the putative victims simply disappeared, knowing full well that particular individuals would spend many years in prison for their "murders." Some people have served long terms in prison for murder only to have their "victims" turn up eventually, alive and well.

Criminal Records

A major factor in the conviction of the innocent is that such defendants often have criminal records. In the case of Robert Daniels, his record probably swayed opinion against him, although it is still difficult to understand how a jury could have found the weight of the evidence so strongly against him that the jurors felt his guilt was established beyond a reasonable doubt. Daniels's case also raises other issues, such as whether the rules of confidentiality should extend to the toleration of so severe a social evil as sending an innocent person to prison—would the therapist have remained silent and allowed the defendant, whom he knew was not guilty, to be executed? If so, this would be ironic, in that physicians are precluded from directly assisting in the execution (even by lethal injection) of guilty offenders, yet a "therapist," claiming "ethical obligations," might remain silent while an innocent man is executed.

A criminal record places a person's picture in police files, where it might possibly be picked out by crime victims. A record also makes an individual more vulnerable to police interrogation and to making false confessions. An innocent defendant with a criminal record is less likely to take the stand to testify in his or her own behalf, because this opens up the possibility that the record will be brought out during cross-examination. If the innocent defendant does not take the stand, he or she is deprived of a witness who can deny the defendant's involvement in the crime. Further, no matter what judges may tell jurors to the contrary, most jurors take a defendant's failure to take the witness stand to be a sign of guilt. Finally, a criminal record makes a witness/defendant suspect once he or she is on the stand. Jurors not only tend to disbelieve a person with a record, they often feel that it is not crucial to determine such a person's guilt or innocence in a given case, because it is good to sweep the bad guys off the streets.

In our source documents, the question of previous criminal record was not mentioned in a sufficient number of cases for us to make a reliable computation, but from following newspaper stories of recent years and from reading books and trial transcripts that go into cases in detail, we know that many convicted innocents have had records that made them vulnerable, and that contributed, with other factors, to their becoming victims of the criminal justice system.

Race as a Factor

Many convicted innocents are white, some are even middle-class, but a disproportionate number are black or Hispanic. Some have been convicted of crimes by all-white, handpicked juries. In the case of George Whitmore, the first conviction of this innocent man was by an all-white jury, and it was only when a journalist heard a rumor, later confirmed in court, that racist language was used in the jury room that the conviction was thrown out. It is difficult to believe that Lenell Geter would have received a guilty verdict, and certainly not a life term, had he not been black. Aside from the prejudices of police, prosecutors, and jurors, being of a race different from that of witnesses may increase the possibility of misidentification.

A miscellany of other factors can work to create convicted innocents. Some are less prevalent and some less investigated than others. These include judicial errors, bias, and neglect of duty; unintentional and sometimes even intentional errors on the part of criminal investigators, medical examiners, and forensic science experts; incompetence of the accused to assist in his or her own defense; and, finally, simple coincidence. All of these factors and others duplicate and overlap one another and synergistically act together. It is a tribute to the criminal justice system if in fact convicted innocents constitute only one-half of 1% of the total number of people convicted each year. It is possible, however, through study, analysis, and proper social policy, to reduce this figure, and it is our contention, as we will show later in this book, that in so doing the criminal justice system will be able to increase the percentage of the guilty who are convicted as well.

The manner in which numerous factors work simultaneously to keep innocent individuals behind bars is dramatically illustrated by an obscure case that surfaced on the front page of the *New York Times* on November 30, 1985. Willie Jones was a 33-year-old black man who had been in minor trouble for lawbreaking in the past, when he was arrested for opening the gate to a New York subway station and attempting to get a ride without paying the fare. Hardly a serious charge, and one might expect that a criminal justice system that had been extraordinarily lenient, almost apologetic, to a white-collar commuter from Connecticut who had been using his Connecticut highway tokens to cheat the New York subways might show a little compassion. But Willie Jones, remanded to jail and referred to legal aid (New York's equivalent of the public defender) for counsel, was confronted with a "rap sheet" that showed a long list of serious crimes, including the revelation that he was now wanted for jumping $3,500 bail.

Over and over, Jones complained to the people at legal aid that the rap sheet was not his, although it bore his name and a physical description not terribly unlike his own. There was no picture and there were no fingerprints, and no one took the trouble to try to obtain these, because everyone knew that the defendant was lying. A plea bargain was arranged between legal aid and the prosecution, but, to the consternation of his attorneys, the accused turned it down, saying that he would not plead guilty to a crime he had not committed. For 3 months, Jones languished in a local jail, until finally the day of his trial arrived. When he came to court, he was greeted by a happy and smiling legal aid counsel who told him that it was all a mistake—he was not the Willie Jones the police (and his own attorneys) had thought he was.

Why did this case take on the form that it did? First, although the charge on which Jones was picked up was very minor, even trivial, the fact was that he was not a model citizen, and although the record the authorities confronted him with was not his own, he did have a previous arrest record. In addition, he was black, and prejudice came into play. There was an assumption that this lower-class black man was making up absurd stories to protest his innocence, when everyone knew he was guilty. Third, he had inadequate counsel, people overburdened with caseloads, anxious to make as many deals as possible in order to get on to their next cases. They had neither the facilities nor the motivation to investigate, demand fingerprints, and look into such a simple matter as the possible difference in social security numbers between two men having the name of Willie Jones. Fourth, he was a victim of plea-bargaining pressure—cop a plea and get the thing over with; move the case through the system; push the widget along the conveyor belt. Fifth, he was a victim of sloppy work, although not malicious, in the police and prosecutorial stages. And sixth, coincidence in part led to Jones's predicament—coincidence plays a part in many cases.

Only one thing separates Willie Jones from the other individuals we discuss in this book: He was never convicted. In his case, the error was discovered before the trial. He was "only" jailed, that's all. A happy ending? Anyone who thinks so has never spent any time in a cramped jail cell with a randomly assigned roommate.

Notes

1. A great deal of information came from the prevalence studies as perceived by Ohio jurists, prosecutors, and others. This information is provided in Table 3.2.

2. The term *index crimes* refers to eight serious crimes that are used as an index of criminality in the United States. Not all serious crimes are considered index crimes, because they are not considered to be reliably reported and are not seen as useful in constructing such an index. The index crimes are as follows: murder and nonnegligent manslaughter, forcible rape, aggravated assault, robbery, burglary, larceny-theft, motor vehicle theft, and arson.

4

What Did They Really See?

The Problems of Eyewitness Identification

On the night of October 12, 1980, a teenage girl became a rape victim after hitchhiking on the Pacific Coast Highway near the Seattle-Tacoma airport. She gave the police a description of her assailant: He was a bearded white man about 6 feet tall, wearing a three-piece, cream-colored suit. He had threatened her with a knife. She had been able to recall something about the car that she had entered: It was a royal blue compact with a temporary license plate displayed in the rear window. She was not certain of all the numbers on the license plate, but she seemed to recall that the first digits were either 667 or 776.

Armed with this information, Port of Seattle police searched the area and came across a bearded man by the name of Steve Gary Titus, who was to become the only suspect in the case. He was driving a light blue Chevette and was spotted by the police outside a restaurant, not far from the rape scene, from which he had just emerged with his fiancée after they had had a drink together. Titus, taken by surprise when approached by the police, was asked a few questions, and then police asked him if he had any objection to his picture being taken. Neither suspicious nor frightened, and certain that he was innocent, he consented without hesitation. He then asked the officers to take an additional picture of him with his girlfriend.

The next day, the 17-year-old rape victim, Celia Dalton, found herself staring at Titus's picture in a photo lineup—a group of six photographs containing front and profile shots of Titus and five other people. Such lineups are supposed to include people of the same race and who are not so markedly different from the suspect that the latter would stand out as the only possible perpetrator. In this case, however, Titus's photos were a different size from those of the other individuals, the only ones showing a smiling face, and the only ones in which the profile and full-face shots were not separated by a black line. Dalton was told before she viewed the photos that the rapist was one of the six men whose photos she would be viewing. After 5 minutes of looking at the photos, she paused, pointed at the pictures of Titus, hesitated a moment, and then said, "This one is the closest one," and then added, "It has to be this one" (Olsen, 1991, p. 169). On the face of it, this was a credible identification. After all, she had come into close confrontation with her assailant, and now she was ready to identify Titus as the man who had raped her on a secluded road near the Seattle-Tacoma airport.

Steve Titus was tried and convicted based on the uncorroborated testimony of the witness, the similarity of his car to the one she had described, and deliberate distortions by a Port Authority police corporal. He remained free on bail while protesting his innocence and waiting for sentence to be imposed, while deeply worried and trying to work on leads for an appeal. He never did go to prison, because his complete exculpation was established before the gates had an opportunity to open and devour him. His innocence was established not through the efforts of the police or the prosecutor, but because of the continuing and relentless efforts of Paul Henderson, a *Seattle Times* reporter, who was convinced that a miscarriage of justice was unfolding before his eyes. The reporter called attention to Titus's airtight alibi, his spotless record, the failure of authorities to conduct proper forensic tests, and the many inconsistencies and errors in the prosecutor's case (some of which had appeared to be remedied by last-minute distortions by the Port Authority corporal). He called for the case to be reopened and insisted on a new investigation.

Ultimately, Titus was exonerated. Eventually, a 28-year-old man was linked to the crime and made a complete confession. When the victim recognized her mistake, she broke down and cried, agonized over having made such a serious error. As we have noted, in many instances of eyewitness error, the innocent accused and the actual perpetrators do not even look alike. However, in this case, there is no question that (as in the Jackson case discussed in Chapter 2) there were similarities between the two in facial appearance and beard, though not in height or preferred style of clothing. Moreover, the actual rapist drove a metallic blue Ford Fiesta hatchback, a car not strikingly different from that same year's Chevette. A young girl untrained in the distinctions that mark one automobile from another might easily confuse the two. And both cars had temporary license plates in their rear windows—a not extraordinarily rare feature.

Steve Titus was more than a victim of wrongful identification. He was a victim of wrongful conviction, though not, mercifully, incarceration or execution. One might think that he may have emerged a hero, with apologies from the authorities and perhaps offers of movie contracts or speaking engagements organized on college campuses, or approaches from feminists anxious to guard against such errors, which in fact injure their cause by giving ammunition to defense attorneys who challenge rape witnesses' credibility. Instead, he found that his and his parents' savings had been depleted by legal fees, a career that had taken him 5 years to build was shattered, and the negative emotional effect on his life had been so overwhelming that he could not seem to gather together the threads and continue on in his career. More than a year after his exoneration, he was drawing unemployment checks and worried that even that income would come to an end soon. Two years later, his fiancée (who never stopped loving him or believing in him) left him because he was no longer the same person she fell in love with. He had been destroyed by his ordeal. In 1985, at the young age of 36, having physically spent himself in the pursuit of justice, Steve Titus died of a massive heart attack. David and Jacqueline Titus, who spent their life savings to exonerate their son, made one final purchase on his behalf, a small bronze plate placed above his grave, which reads:

Our Beloved Son Steve G. Titus
1949–1985
He Fought for His Day in Court
He Was Used, Deceived, Betrayed
And Denied Justice Even in Death
(quoted in Olsen, 1991, p. 389)

The only person who emerged unscathed from (but profoundly affected by) Steve Titus's ordeal was Paul Henderson, the reporter who deservedly won a Pulitzer Prize for his work on the case. Even he was not uniformly admired, however. Many law enforcement officers, instead of expressing gratitude to Henderson for helping correct an error and helping take a serial rapist off the streets, treated him as persona non grata. The professionalism Henderson exhibited stood in stark contrast to the Port Authority's lack of integrity in this case.

The Titus case is of special interest because (a) all of the key people involved in the conviction were white, thus eliminating any question of racial prejudice; (b) Titus did not have a criminal record that might have required his lawyer to ask him not to take the stand or might have convinced jurors that they were dealing with an evil person who ought to be convicted even on flimsy evidence; (c) he had an airtight alibi; and (d) there were many inadequacies and inconsistencies in the prosecutor's case. In short, this was hardly a case in which one could have expected conviction based on proof beyond a reasonable doubt. But it was certainly not the first case, nor will it be the last, in which eyewitness identification, made in good faith, has led to the conviction of an entirely innocent person. In the Titus case, the power of the eyewitness was further magnified by the prosecutor's courtroom theatrics. He asked the victim to show the jury how close she had been to the offender, and when she walked over to the defense table to demonstrate, the jury could see her agony with each step she took, because she was convinced that Titus was the man who had raped her.

Although eyewitnesses have long been considered the eyes and ears of justice, these essential organs of perception can be most defective. Criminal justice experts have long observed that eyewitness identification is often perceived as the most convincing part of a trial, and in its absence, defense attorneys often mount tirades against what is called, often disparagingly, *circumstantial evidence.* On the other hand, criminal justice experts also report that these eyes and ears can be most deceptive. Research indicates that a substantial number of errors resulting in the conviction of innocent persons emanate from what can be termed good-faith eyewitness identification, and that is particularly important when there is an interracial identification, whether or not overt and conscious prejudice is involved. Rattner (1983) reports that more than 52% of the false convictions he examined involved misidentification, although other factors were usually present as well (in the Titus case, for example, the similarity of the automobile and the unethical conduct of the police cannot be overlooked). Borchard (1932) reports that eyewitness error contributed to 45% of the wrongful convictions in his sample. And although Bedau and Radelet (1987) found eyewitness error to be a factor in only 16% of their cases, we believe this finding is a result of sampling differences, because these researchers focused solely on capital or potentially capital cases, which, by their very nature, are less likely to involve eyewitnesses.

The various factors contributing to the unreliability of eyewitness identification have been explored by a number of researchers (e.g., Buckhout, Figueroa, & Hoff, 1975; Clifford & Scott, 1978; Loftus, 1979). Our analysis of such studies and our own database indicates that the factors contributing to misidentification can be collapsed into three major categories. First, there are psychological factors emanating from the disturbed emotional state (or even shock) of the witness or bystander. Such trauma may exacerbate an individual's already imperfect powers of perception, the difficulty of retaining information during stressful situations, and the inability to retrieve such information from the memory's storage system. Second, there are systemic factors related to the various functions of the criminal justice system. These include the procedures used for mug shot and lineup identifications and the suggestions that may be introduced during investigation in the time leading up to and during identification. Third, there are flaws in eyewitness identification stemming from societal and cultural expectations and difficulties with cross-racial identification, which may introduce confusion even where no prejudice exists. All three of these factors contribute to the unreliability of eyewitness identification and pose serious problems for the administration of criminal justice, particularly inasmuch as convictions of the guilty cannot easily be obtained without such eyewitness reports.

Psychological Factors

When a person experiences an important event, he or she does not simply record that event in memory, as would a videotape recorder.

Theoretical analysis of how perception becomes memory divides the process into three stages (Loftus, 1979, pp. 20-110):

1. *Acquisition:* the perception of the original event in which information is encoded, laid down, or entered into a person's memory system
2. *Retention:* the period of time that passes between the event and the moment when the individual is called upon to recollect a particular piece of information
3. *Retrieval:* the phase during which the individual actually brings back to consciousness and, usually, makes known to others the stored information

Various factors have important impacts on the human memory during the occurrence of complex events. In the acquisition stage of memory, the brain of the observer makes decisions as to which aspects of the visual stimulus merit attention and focus. An incredibly large number of bits and pieces of sights and sounds surround us at almost all times, and during frightening or traumatic events, or incidents that pass quickly before our eyes, we are able to note only a minute percentage of what visually confronts us. Very little is known about the hierarchy of factors that influence unconscious decisions about what we retain in memory after moments of stress. We cannot retain and store every image we are exposed to during the acquisition stage. Further, particular activities can cause powerful and unexpected changes in the functioning of the memory, usually working to reduce retention, but sometimes enhancing it. Retention of memories is of course linked to length of time since an event in the normal, well-functioning brain, and some details, which may or may not be the most significant, are retained far longer than others. Retrieval of items from memory is influenced not only by information acquired during the original event, but also by what has occurred in the intervening period of retention and by the circumstances of the moment when one is called to make known what has been retrieved (Crowder, 1976).

The processes of memory acquisition, retention, and retrieval are strongly influenced by the *event factors* (Loftus, 1979) inherent in an incident—for example, the amount of exposure time, the light or darkness, and the distance of the observer from what he or she is perceiving. Research indicates that the less time a witness has to look at something or to be exposed to an event, the less accurate his or her perception will be. For example, in one of the earliest studies in this area, Whipple (1909) found that an eyewitness should be able to recall an event more accurately when the event transpires and is observed over a longer period of time. Such commonsense and obvious conclusions are often overlooked in court by the side trying to impeach a witness's credibility, yet, like other truisms, have required and successfully obtained substantiation in scientific research.

Laughery, Alexander, and Lane (1971) conducted an experiment designed to measure the ability of subjects to identify a target face 8 minutes after they had been exposed to its picture. One group was exposed to this picture for a period of 10 seconds; the other group had the same view, from the same distance and with the same light, for 32 seconds. As expected, subjects who had viewed the face longer were somewhat more accurate, successfully identifying the face in 75% of cases, as contrasted with only 47% accuracy by those who had viewed the same face for the shorter time. Actually, there were two time factors at work in this study: exposure time and lapse of time between exposure and identification. The fact that the latter was so short, only 8 minutes, makes the results obtained all the more striking.

Given the types of offenses represented in our study (45% involve murder; 12.2%, forcible rape; and 30.5%, robbery) and the increasing demands on urban police forces, it is hardly surprising that the elapsed time between a criminal act and the questioning of a victim or another witness will almost always exceed 8 minutes. In addition, where conviction is based in part on a lineup or in-court identification, these procedures may occur weeks, even months, after the crime has been committed.

Research on eyewitness identification has produced compelling evidence that postevent information can have an even more detrimental impact than elapsed time on the memory's retention and retrieval ability. Loftus, Miller, and Burns (1978) gave information that could be considered similar to leading and nonleading questions during an investigation to subjects in both "immediate" and "delayed" sequences. They found that when information was given immediately after an event, correct performance was quite high, with almost 90% accuracy. The level of performance dropped gradually as the time interval increased, and after a period of 2 days, subjects were performing at about 50% accuracy (as Loftus et al. indicate, many were probably simply guessing at that point). In the same experiment, the researchers also introduced both leading and misleading information. They found that when subjects were given leading information consistent with the event, 70% were correct in their retrieval of the event. In contrast, when subjects received misleading information—information inconsistent with the event—only 20% of the subjects were correct in their retrieval (this part of the experiment took place one week after the event). Of this work, Loftus (1979) states:

> This experiment shows that in general, longer retention intervals lead to worse performance; consistent information improves performance and misleading information hinders it; and misleading information that is given immediately after an event has less of an impact on the memory than misleading information that is delayed until just prior to the test. (p. 66)

In addition, many factors inherent in incidents themselves, or event factors, have been found to reduce witnesses' abilities to report and identify accurately. Several researchers have analyzed and isolated the types of details and types of events that may affect memory acquisition, retention, and retrieval (e.g., Buckhout et al., 1975). Such factors as the height and weight of a suspect, the amount of time an incident lasts (exposure time), and the color and shape of significant objects (such as an automobile) have been found to be unequal in subjects' ease of perception and recall. These findings tend to indicate the probability of witnesses' making errors in estimating the duration of incidents and in describing the height, weight, shape, and color of other persons. The problems that occur in the initial perceptions of such information can later cause difficulties in the retrieval of the information.

Whether an event is violent or nonviolent has a significant effect on witnesses' ability to recall it. Clifford and Scott (1978) found that, among their subjects, the ability to recall events with detail and accuracy was far inferior for those who had witnessed a violent rather than a nonviolent act. They conclude that testimony about an emotionally loaded incident should be treated with greater caution than testimony about an event that has caused less trauma to the witness. Thus, the victims or witnesses of the most violent acts have the highest likelihood of misidentifying the perpetrators involved.

Along somewhat similar lines, Leippe, Weil, and Ostrom (1978) argue that the seriousness of a crime might influence eyewitness accuracy (of course, seriousness and violence are usually linked). These researchers suggest that motivating effects have an impact on the memory encoding process. In other words, a witness to a serious crime may have greater motivation to attend actively to the physical appearance of the perpetrator than would a witness to a crime that appears to be trivial or innocuous. However, a witness to a serious crime, particularly a violent crime, may have a greater desire to remain uninvolved than would a witness to a trivial crime. Thus, the paradox: A witness may be motivated by a serious criminal event to pay active attention to the perpetrator and yet, in order to remain uninvolved and not alert the perpetrator to the presence of a potential witness, may actually pay less attention than he or she would to a less serious crime, or may even turn away and seek to ignore the culprit.

The factors that contribute to unreliable witness testimony also affect disinterested witnesses, bystanders, and victims. Stress has been found to be an important factor influencing human beings' ability to perceive complex events; crime witnesses often experience stress during criminal events, because they often perceive themselves to be in grave danger. The human body responds to such stress with increases in heart rate, respiration, and blood pressure, and a dramatic increase in the flow of adrenalin and thus of available energy, enhancing the person's "fight or flight" capabilities to ensure survival (Buckhout, 1974). Studies of behavior have tended to show that people have diminished ability to remember details of events that occurred when they were experiencing extreme stress. Under such conditions, contrary to the belief of many judges, perception and memory are usually inaccurate (*People v. Johnson,* 1974). Aside from the influences of stress on the acquisition of memory, a witness who is in a state of intense fear may tend to focus on weapons or escape routes rather than on a criminal's face or physical characteristics.

Ellison and Buckhout (1981) indicate that even among highly trained people, powers of observation deteriorate under stress. Moreover, whereas experimental evidence shows no difference between police and civilians in face recognition ability, it also shows that police officers are especially prone to perceive suspicious behavior as intent to commit crime and may therefore justify these perceptions by "remembering" events that have not happened.

Stress, fright, and trauma are not the only conditions that can contribute to the unreliability of memory function. Witnesses who are old, sick, tired, or under the influence of alcohol may suffer from various dysfunctions that can influence the accuracy of their memories.

Among the factors influencing memory retention are the passage of time and reminders or reviews of an event. Illness during the period after an event, other important events in life, changes in personal situation, hypnosis, and other intervening variables may affect both retention and retrieval of memories. Exposure to similar people or events after a given event may adversely affect retention of memories about that event, cause confusion, and even lead to some partial amnesia. Repeated suggestions by others about an event, such as badgering by police and prosecutors that they cannot proceed with witness statements of "I think" or "That is probably the one," but only with "I know" or "I am sure" or "I am certain," can lead a witness actually to believe in the certainty of his or her identification (not merely to assert such a belief). All such factors can affect a witness's memory and, in some cases, even cause nonexistent details to become incorporated into previously acquired information.

For witnesses, the retrieval of information from memory occurs most frequently in the context of interaction with those who are in charge of obtaining the accounts of an event for the criminal justice system. An important focus at this stage is the relationship between communicating with the witness and retrieving the information. In an early study of memory retrieval, Feingold (1914) found that changing the setting and the environmental condition, from the original crime scene to the place where the investigation of the lineup takes place, might affect recognition. In his conclusion, Feingold suggests that "the proper way to obtain a successful recognition is not to bring the witness into the police station but to bring the supposed lawbreaker to the scene of the crime and have the [witness] look at him precisely in the same surroundings and from the same angle at which he saw them originally" (p. 42). Much has occurred since Feingold made this suggestion, of course; today it may be considered more prejudicial than helpful to an innocent person to be viewed in the context of the crime scene. Nonetheless, there is a possibility that light and darkness, angles, distance, and other aspects surrounding the event might influence the certainty articulated by the eyewitness reviewing a police lineup. Certainly Feingold's suggestion would be ridiculed today.

Systemic Factors

Our concern up to this point has been with psychological factors of eyewitness identification and their interaction with the criminal justice system. However, these are not the only variables contributing to good-faith false identification. What can be called systemic factors may also play a critical role. Several other modes of identification, in addition to traditional lineups, exemplify the entire gamut of systemic factors and contribute to the skepticism with which one must view the testimony of eyewitnesses. These are illustrated in the case of *Delaware v. Pagano* (1979). Most of the material regarding the process of eyewitness identification in this case has been analyzed at length by Robert Buckhout, who served as the major expert witness. Precisely because "no glaring constitutional errors would conflict with the then existing law," to use Buckhout's language, the gross miscarriage of justice in the misidentification of Father Pagano illustrates dramatically how systemic factors contribute to this type of error.

After a series of armed robberies in the state of Delaware, the police were able to construct a composite drawing of the perpetrator. At that point, anonymous callers alerted the police that the drawing looked very much like a Catholic priest, Father Vincent Pagano, who was not in favor with many higher persons in his own church. Based on these anonymous tips, the priest was kept under surveillance, and at a certain point in the investigation the police brought two eyewitnesses with them while they staked out a club where they had been told Father Pagano would be at that particular time. Indeed, he was there, and when he emerged from the club, the police and the witnesses moved closer to him so they could all get a good view. The priest, completely innocent and not suspecting that he was being watched by police or strangers, took little notice of what was occurring. Later, Buckhout would testify that this type of one-on-one "show-up" has an error potential of 50% and is inherently biased, because witnesses are given no other choice except to say either yes or no; that is, they cannot pick out one person among five or six. Some witnesses feel an internal pressure to make an identification, in order to avoid disappointing or displeasing the police.

The next stage in the Pagano identification involved two photo lineups. In both, the photos of the other men differed significantly in age, hairstyle, and clothing from that of the priest, who had become the prime suspect. As a final step, a lineup was conducted in which seven of the eight witnesses positively identified Father Pagano. Finally, during the in-court identification, all witnesses identified the defendant, who was ordered to stand trial for armed robbery and who subsequently was once again identified, this time in front of a jury, by all witnesses who were called.

An in-depth analysis conducted by Buckhout (1979) in collaboration with the defense attorneys emphasizes the following points:

1. The composite drawings prepared by the police and published in the local newspaper might have created some problematic conditions. In those cases where a witness has only a fragmentary description of the criminal and some vital items in his or her memory are missing, he or she might, under pressure from the investigator, complete these missing items. Literature on this subject indicates that in such instances witnesses tend to complete images in a stereo-typed manner (stereotyped details of a suspect's hairstyle, expression, and the like) (see Buckhout & Greenwald, 1980). This image, when widely disseminated, will cause people, including other potential witnesses, to fill in the description and match it to their memories.

2. One-on-one show-ups such as that conducted during this investigation are inherently unreliable. Wall (1965) describes this method as the most grossly suggestive identification procedure ever used by the police. Despite the high degree of suggestion that exists when such an identification is taking place, the courts have in many cases affirmed convictions based on this method. Defendants have been brought, handcuffed, in front of witnesses, who were told not to worry about making an identification when confronted alone in a room with the suspect (see *People v. Barad,* 1936; *People v. Kind,* 1934; *State v. Landeros,* 1955). The Supreme Court has indicated also, in *Stovall v. Denno* (1967), that "the practice of showing suspects singly to persons for the purpose of identification, and not as part of a lineup, has been widely condemned."

3. Photo identification may also incorporate a great deal of suggestion. Pagano's photo was included along with photos of eight other men who differed from him in significant respects (clothing, hairstyle,

and age). The background in Pagano's photo was also distinct from all the others.

4. The series of lineups conducted shortly before the opening of the trial, although seemingly fair and reasonable, with the defendant represented by counsel, apparently involved bias in that the attention of the witness was directed to the suspect. Pagano was standing in the lineup with his hands folded, a possible nonverbal cue to his priestly status, when of course all witnesses knew at that time that the defendant was a priest. The fact that the photo of the defendant had been shown to all witnesses more than once created major bias in the process of identification, because it became impossible to ascertain whether an identification emanated from the witness's memory of the crime or from the witness's frequent viewing of the picture.

Just as the true perpetrator confessed on the day Steve Titus was to be sentenced, it was on the morning that Buckhout was waiting to be called as an expert witness on eyewitness identification that another man appeared in court, charged with several robberies, and confessed to the robberies and burglaries attributed to Pagano. The actual perpetrator bore a striking resemblance to Pagano.

Several issues that pose serious problems to the functioning of the criminal justice system are suggested by the Pagano case, as well as other cases involving errors of eyewitness identification, although technically Pagano never reached the moment of conviction.

Although only a little more than 3% of the cases in our database emanated from an initial identification of the suspect through a mug shot, this source of error is particularly troubling. The U.S. Supreme Court, in *United States v. Williams* (1979), has indicated that even if such an identification begins as a permissible procedure, it might later, at the stage of arrest, affect the lineup. Thus, in *Simmons v. United States* (1968), the majority stated:

> It must be recognized that improper employment of photographs by police may sometimes cause witnesses to err in identifying criminals. A witness may have obtained only a brief glance at a criminal, or may have seen him under poor conditions. . . . This danger will be

increased if the police display to the witness only the picture of a single individual who generally resembles the person he saw, or if they show him the pictures of several persons among which the photograph of a single such individual recurs or is in some ways emphasized. The chance of misidentification is also heightened if the police indicate to the witness that they have other evidence that one of the person's pictures [is the photograph of the individual who] committed the crime. Regardless of how the initial misidentification comes about, the witness therefore is apt to retain in his memory the image of the photograph rather than of the person actually seen, reducing the trustworthiness of subsequent lineup.

Nevertheless, the Court in this case did not rule out the use of photo identification. It stated that "a conviction based on eyewitness identification at the trial, following a pretrial identification of a photograph, will be set aside only if the photographic identification procedure was so impermissibly suggestive as to give rise to a very substantial likelihood of irreparable misidentification" (*Simmons v. United States,* 1968, p. 377). In a later case, the Court indicated that the common police practice of showing witnesses photographs of the suspect before conducting an actual lineup reduces reliability (*Bennet v. State,* 1975).

Researchers have noted that the process of having a witness or an eyewitness search through a mug shot album of photos compiled by police might impair the person's memory. Davies, Shepherd, and Hadyn (1979) have demonstrated in a series of experiments that the accuracy of face recognition is significantly affected by exposure to earlier pictorial stimuli. The main concern with regard to photo identification is that any corporeal identification of the accused might actually be based on the victim's or witness's recollection of the photo and not his or her memory of the person actually seen perpetrating a crime.

Brown, Defenbacker, and Sturgill (1977) conducted an experiment in this area that yielded dramatic results. In this study, which was a simulation of a photo identification and a lineup, subjects viewed a group of "criminals" and were told that they would be required to pick them out from mug shots and a lineup. An hour after they viewed the criminals, the subjects were shown mug shots; a week later, they were asked to participate in a lineup identification. The results indicate that of those persons who had not been seen before, 8% were wrongly identified. However, when a person's picture was earlier presented as a mug shot, his chances of being wrongly identified increased to 20%.

In the second stage of the experiment, the subjects viewed the putative criminals without being told that they would have to identify them later. Under these circumstances, among those who were not seen before, 18% were wrongly identified; more strikingly, among those whose mug shots were presented prior to the lineup, 29% were erroneously chosen. Loftus (1979) attributes the problem of photo-based lineup identification to the general problem of unconscious transference. The identified person in a lineup will look familiar simply because his or her photo was seen earlier, and this familiarity may be mistakenly related to the crime rather than to the photo identification.

An alternate form of identification is the lineup, which can and does lead to error even when no photograph has been previously shown. Although many legal experts and researchers claim that a fairly conducted lineup is the best available method of accurate pretrial identification, there are some hazards of mistaken identification associated with this method. A major source of bias is introduced when a victim or witness is informed that the suspect is in the lineup. These dynamics were present, in part, in the identification of Father Pagano, because extensive publicity was given to the suspect prior to his lineup identification. In other cases, lineups may be held several months after the crimes were committed, and because memory retention and retrieval are influenced by the passage of time, can therefore lead to misidentifications.

Still other circumstances can lead to lineups being suggestive and biased, such as dissimilarity between a suspect's physical appearance and that of the other individuals in the lineup. Among the most flagrant examples of this kind of problem, now diminishing in the United States but once rather common, is the lineup in which the suspect is of one racial group and some of the other members of the lineup are of another (Wall, 1965).

By far the most serious problem with lineup identification occurs once an identification has been made (however hesitant the witness may be). At that point, all adversaries and some neutral figures in the criminal justice system (police, prosecutor, judge, jury, and even the lawyer for the defense) may become convinced of the defendant's guilt, the possibility of error notwithstanding. The police and prosecutor, already convinced of the suspect's guilt, begin to be driven by *deductive* logic and strengthen their case by urging that the witness not show uncertainty. Many witnesses themselves do not like to appear uncertain of the accuracy of what they are testifying to, and become convinced that there is no lingering doubt.

Wall (1965) discusses the dangers and absurdities inherent in lineup identifications:

> Lawyers who have had experience with police "lineups" are perfectly familiar with the fact that mistakes in identification are very frequent. Time and again witnesses bona fide identify persons in a "lineup" as the offender, when such persons could not possibly have partici-pated in the offense, because they were in jail when the offense was committed. But often the accused man has been unlucky in not being in jail when the offense was committed and therefore unable to furnish such an ironclad alibi. (p. 64)

Sagarin (1975) makes extraordinarily similar remarks, except that he describes an identification made from the photographs in the rogues' gallery:

> An instance of false identification is recounted by a staunch defender of the women's liberation thrust on rape. According to this writer [Grace Lichstenstein, in the *New York Times*], a woman was forcibly raped by two men who were complete strangers to her. At the police headquarters, she was shown photographs of many men, and finally came to one. This was the younger of the two perpetrators, she said. The detectives had hit pay dirt! Was she sure? She was 95 percent positive. All one had to do was to find the culprit. Alas, he was in prison, where he had been on the day of the offense. (p. 134)

Societal and Cultural Factors

Studies concerning individuals' ability to recognize and identify faces that differ from their own, and certainly those of people of other races, strongly challenge the likelihood of accurate witness identification of criminal suspects. In a series of experiments, Malpass and Kravitz (1969) attempted to obtain two measures of recognition: the number of correct identifications and the number of false identifications. Among their subjects, more false identifications were made concerning persons of other racial groups than were made concerning subjects' own racial groups. In a study conducted by Brigham and Barkowitz (1978), the following findings emerged:

1. False identifications were more common when both blacks and whites identified members of the other race.
2. The errors and false identifications further increased when cross-racial identifications were made by highly prejudiced people.
3. Experience with persons of the other race reduced the number of false identifications.

Thus, empirical research on the factors affecting the accuracy of personal identification has focused on cross-racial factors as well as on the common situation of eyewitness identification within a given racial or ethnic group.

As we have noted, the various factors contributing to the unreliability of eyewitness identification have been explored by many researchers (e.g., Buckhout et al., 1975; Clifford & Scott, 1978; Loftus, 1979; Shapiro & Penrod, 1986). To summarize, three major types of factors have been identified that may influence eyewitness identification. First are the psychological factors that can emanate from the disturbed emotional state of the victim or bystander; such trauma may exacerbate a human being's already imperfect powers of perception and the difficulty of retaining and retrieving information stored in memory during stressful situations. Second are systemic factors related to the various functions of the criminal justice system. These include the procedures used for mug shot and lineup identifications that can lead to false identifications. Third, and of interest in this section, are factors related to societal and cultural expectations and cross-racial identification.

A meta-analysis of facial identification studies reveals that only 13% of the studies on eyewitness identification have used both black and white targets (Shapiro & Penrod, 1986). A careful review of these studies and experiments reveals some conflicting findings. Two early studies conducted by Cross, Cross, and Daley (1971) and Malpass and Kravitz (1969) conclude that own-race bias is limited to white subjects—white subjects recognized pictures of white people better than they did pictures of black people, whereas black subjects recognized pictures of whites and blacks at similar rates. Later studies, however, have indicated that own-race bias exists at about the same rates among blacks and whites (e.g., Brigham & Barkowitz, 1978; Chance, Goldstein, & McBride, 1975). In their summary of 14 studies of racial bias in identification, Brigham and Malpass (1985) conclude that, on the average, both black and white people recognize faces of their own races better than faces of other races.

Similar identification studies have employed, among others, American Indian, Chinese American, and Japanese American subjects. All of these studies have found that rates of false identification are higher when subjects are asked to identify members of races other than their own (e.g., Brigham & Barkowitz, 1978; Luce, 1974). Although these findings force the conclusion that people have greater difficulty recognizing target faces of other races than they have recognizing target faces of their own, investigators have not provided any plausible explanation for this phenomenon. Researchers have examined various mediating factors in their attempts to determine what may affect cross-racial recognition ability. Two factors frequently mentioned are racial attitudes and extent of interracial contact. It has been hypothesized that highly prejudiced persons are less accurate in identifying people of other races, and that those who have had more contact with members of other races may be more accurate in other-race identification (Brigham & Barkowitz, 1978). Neither assumption has received sufficient support, however. Brigham and Barkowitz (1978) have asserted that although both whites and blacks perform better in own-race than in other-race identification, neither their racial attitudes nor the extent of their interracial experience is related to their recognition ability.

Another explanation for other-race misidentification is that people who belong to a particular race tend to have distinctive features (for example, characteristic complexion, eye shape, hair texture), so that when, for instance, a non-Asian observes an Asian person, those distinctive features stand out and consume a great deal of the identifier's processing time. When the observer is later confronted with an array of Asian faces, their common features are of little help to him or her in discriminating among specific Asian faces (Loftus, 1979).

Other researchers have suggested that highly distinctive faces are more easily recognized than less distinctive faces, an assumption confirmed by

Going and Read (1974). Seelman (1940) sums up the whole issue by citing the popular conviction that "they [members of races other than one's own] all look alike." The empirical research into factors affecting the accuracy of personal identification has focused almost entirely on the cross-racial factor.

A recent study by Rattner, Weimann, and Fishman (1987) is the first of its kind, to our knowledge, to examine the problem of misidentification beyond the racial context—specifically, by examining the problem of misidentification from the cross-ethnic perspective in Israeli society. Israel furnishes an ideal setting for studying questions concerning ethnic groups. The massive immigration of Jews from all over the world has produced a highly mixed population in terms of ethnic origins. This population may be broadly divided into Ashkenazic (of European origin) and Sephardic (coming from countries in Asia and North Africa) groups. The country also has a large Arab minority living alongside the two Jewish ethnic groups. It should also be noted that Sephardic Jews generally have darker complexions than Ashkenazic Jews and often resemble Arabs more than they do their Ashkenazic brethren, who tend to have a more "European" appearance.

Because of its social and cultural pluralism, Israeli society is a natural laboratory for investigating the effects of ethnic identification and physiognomic heterogeneity upon the accuracy of cross-ethnic identification. The procedure utilized in the experiment conducted by Rattner et al. involved presenting a sample of 513 subjects (males and females of Ashkenazic, Sephardic, and Arabic origin) with a series of facial photos of people from ethnic groups other than their own. After the subjects examined the pictures, they were asked to identify the same faces from a larger set of pictures containing photos of Ashkenazic, Sephardic, and Arabic persons. Two types of errors were analyzed in this study: nonidentification (the inability to identify a picture that was shown earlier) and false identification (the incorrect identification of a picture that had not been shown earlier). The findings of this study demonstrate clearly that members of the sample population had a 30% chance of not being identified and a similar chance of being falsely identified by a random sample of identifiers. Log-linear analysis clearly showed that the ethnicity of the identifier has the strongest effect on the frequency of both nonidentification and false identification. In the case of false identification, the ethnicity of the identified yielded a highly significant and strong effect when photos of Arabs had to be identified; Arabs had the highest chance of being falsely identified. Although the relationship between cross-ethnic recognition ability and ethnic stereotypes was not the subject of this study, the authors suggest that the high rates of false identification of Arabs can be associated with negative attitudes toward and stereotypes of Arabs.

Such studies indicate that the more heterogeneous a society becomes, the more difficulties its members have in cross-racial identification, the very reverse of what common sense might suggest. Therefore, the chances of wrongful conviction due to misidentification probably increase under modern conditions of mass migration, geographic mobility, and, in the United States at least, rather open borders.

In addition to the impact of cross-racial identification, there is the question of expectations—that is, the tendency of people to see what they want to see, or what they need to see, in order to satisfy themselves. Loftus (1979) identifies four types of expectations that have an impact on perception:

1. Cultural expectations or stereotypes
2. Expectations from past experience
3. Personal prejudices
4. Momentary and temporary expectations

Cultural expectations are the beliefs held by large numbers of people within a cultural context. Allport and Postman (1974) indicate that most people file away some stereotypes, on the basis of which they make perceptual judgments; thus, stereotypes lead not only to prejudice but to more efficient decision making. These researchers showed subjects a scene of a New York subway train filled with many people. Two men in the picture were standing and talking to each other, a black man wearing a tie and a white man holding a razor blade. More than half of all respondents who were asked to report their perceptions of the photo after it had been removed from their view indicated that it was the black man who held the razor in his hand. We have informally shown this photo to people and have found that their reactions, when confronted with the realization that they identified the black man erroneously, have often been profound. This type of demonstration is one of the most effective techniques we know of for illustrating how racial prejudices and stereotypes may distort perception and memory. We believe that similar exercises should be used in training sessions with law enforcement personnel, prosecutors, and judges to help them gain a greater appreciation of the complexities and hazards of eyewitness recall and identification.

Expectations are based on the important role that past experience plays in perception. For example, two men are seen leaving the scene of an apartment they have just burglarized. A witness gets a close view of one of the men and recognizes him as an acquaintance. Although she does not get as good a look at the other man, she identifies him as a very close friend of the first man. This hypothetical case, described by Loftus (1979), indicates how expectations based on past experience may lead to mistaken identification.

In a more recent Israeli experiment, Fishman, Rattner, and Weimann (1987) investigated the impact of ethnic origin on the attribution of criminal offenses to faces seen in portrait photographs. Their findings indicate that the impact of ethnicity as a form of categorization clearly reflects the social climate. They found that Israeli Arabs were more likely than other groups to be identified as criminals, and that more serious crimes were attributed to them. At the other end of the spectrum, Ashkenazic Jews were less likely than members of the other groups to have crimes attributed to them; indeed, the only crime attributed to them was fraud.

The findings of this study have theoretical, methodological, and practical implications. On the theoretical level, the findings underscore the important effect of ethnicity on labeling behavior. The ethnicity of the individual in a portrait was the most powerful variable in determining the attribution of offenses; it was the major factor in attributing crimes, even more powerful than either the expressed attitudes of subjects toward other groups or the subjects' extent of the contact with them. This supports the argument, suggested by attribution theory, that people have well-established sets of social categories that they use in making attributions both to other people and to situations (Brislin, 1990). This behavior is by no means confined to Israeli society. There have been a number of studies of the relations between ethnicity and stereotyping in other societies (for review, see Brigham, 1981) and its impact on judgment concerning guilt and innocence (e.g., Shoemaker, South, & Lowe, 1973). The main contribution of the Israeli study is that it highlights the correspondence between ethnic dominance and attribution processes.

Conclusion

Despite the serious problems and hazards caused by the use of eyewitness identification in the criminal justice system, officials tend to rate eyewitness testimony as the most crucial kind of evidence that can brought to trial (Lavrakas & Bickman, 1975). Brigham (1981) reports the findings of an analysis based on a questionnaire mailed to criminal justice officials in the state of Florida. The questionnaire was designed to estimate how frequently attorneys are involved with various identification procedures and how frequently mistakes of eyewitness identification occur and to examine the relationship between identification accuracy and witness certainty. The mailing went to public defenders, attorneys in state's attorneys' offices in 20 state judicial circuits, and a sample of private criminal defense attorneys. Of the respondents, 59% of the attorneys in state's attorneys' offices, 42% of those in public defenders' offices, and 7% of private criminal lawyers indicated that they were involved in photo lineups once a week or more. Live lineups were encountered much less often; less than 7% of the entire sample experienced live lineups once a week or more.

By inference, based on nothing more than how common it is to use such eyewitness identification procedures, our criminal justice system may face an increasing number and rate of erroneous identifications and a corresponding elevation in the probability of convicting innocent men and women. Our survey (see Chapter 3) indicates that 78.4% of our respondents ranked witness error as the most frequent type of error resulting in wrongful conviction; within that category, 60.4% ranked "accidental eyewitness misidentification" as the most frequent error: a clear indication that few cases are believed to result from deliberate perjury or bad-faith testimony in the identification of defendants. Even though the gatekeepers of the system (prosecutors and judges) ranked eyewitness misidentification as the most frequent error (62.5% of the judges and 84.1% of the prosecutors), it is nonetheless generally looked upon as the most crucial kind of evidence that can be brought in a criminal trial.

Before 1967, the U.S. Supreme Court had not addressed the difficulties and hazards associated with eyewitness identification. Then three cases before the Court were handled in a single decision, with diverse opinions and dissents. These cases, which we discussed briefly in Chapter 3, came to be known as the Wade trilogy: *United States v. Wade* (1967), *Gilbert v.*

California (1967), and *Stovall v. Denno* (1967). The concern of the Court regarding eyewitness identification is reflected in this excerpt:

> The vagaries of eyewitness identification are well known; the annals of criminal law are rife with instances of mistaken identification. . . . A major factor contributing to the high incidence of miscarriage of justice from mistaken identification has been the degree of suggestion inherent in the manner in which the prosecution presents a suspect to witnesses for identification. A commentator has observed that the instance of improper suggestion upon identifying witnesses probably accounts for more miscarriages of justice than any other single factor—perhaps it is responsible for more errors than all other factors combined. . . . Suggestions can be created intentionally or unintentionally in many subtle ways. And the dangers for the suspect are particularly grave when the witness's opportunity for observation was insubstantial, and thus, his susceptibility to suggestion the greatest.

In another case, that of *Jackson v. Fogg* (1978), Judge Lumbard of the Second Circuit Court stated:

> Centuries of experience in the administration of criminal justice have shown that convictions based solely on testimony that identifies a defendant previously unknown to the witness is highly suspect. Of the various kinds of evidence, it is the least reliable, especially where unsupported by corroborating evidence.

In the Wade case, the defendant was charged with robbery of a federally insured bank. Although a defense attorney was appointed to represent the defendant, FBI agents arranged a lineup without notifying the attorney. Wade was identified by two witnesses, both of them bank employees, who testified later in court that the defendant Wade was the man who held up the bank. An appeal was filed after conviction on the ground that the attorney was not present at the pretrial identification. Wade's conviction was reversed by the U.S. Court of Appeals for the Fifth Circuit, which indicated that a verdict of guilt based on a lineup in the absence of the defense attorney violates the Sixth Amendment right to counsel. The U.S. Court of Appeals, to which the case went next, expressed concern about the problems and dangers of eyewitness identification. The court indicated that because show-ups and lineups are critical stages in the pretrial process, the suspect is entitled to have counsel present at those stages. This, the court stated, is necessary in order to avoid or reduce any element of suggestion in a police lineup and therefore to minimize the chances of identifying the wrong person.

In *Gilbert v. California,* the Supreme Court examined whether the in-court identification of the defendant was tainted by a lineup identification that had been conducted by the police without notice to the defendant's counsel. The Court decided to grant Gilbert a new trial and, in doing so, indicated that if the prosecution introduces an unfair, tainted lineup identification during the trial, it cannot be allowed a later opportunity to demonstrate that this testimony had an independent source.

The third case in the trilogy is *Stovall v. Denno,* in which the defendant was appealing a conviction of murder and a sentence of death. A man and his wife were attacked, the man killed, the wife stabbed and hospitalized for surgery. In the hospital, the survivor identified Stovall as the assailant when he was brought, handcuffed, to her bedside. He was black, as had been the murderer, and he was alone as a suspect; there was no lineup. The widow later recovered and made a positive identification in her testimony in court. In this particular case the prosecution defended the one-man show-up on the grounds of circumstantial imperative, particularly the possibility that the witness might die. The court, however, held that unnecessarily suggestive procedures may lead to a denial of due process. A pretrial identification must be excluded if (a) the identification procedure was so suggestive as to violate due process, (b) no exigent circumstances existed to justify the suggestive procedure, or (c) the prosecution is unable to show that the courtroom identification originated independent of the impermissible suggestive procedure (Woocher, 1977).

The safeguards against eyewitness misidentification erected in the Wade trilogy have been eroded by the same criminal justice system that built them. In *Kirby v. Illinois* (1972), a majority of the Supreme Court affirmed Kirby's conviction on robbery charges and held that the right to counsel, as initiated by *Wade,* is applicable only after a formal indictment or arraignment. Kirby had been arrested, along with a companion, and taken to a police station. Some items that were found in his possession had been stolen in a recent robbery. One of the robbery witnesses who was brought to the station house identified the suspects as the robbers; Kirby had not yet been indicted for the crime, and no attorney was present during the identification. At a later trial in Illinois, where the crime and the arrests occurred, the defendants were again identified by the victim; this testimony was crucial in the prosecution's case, and led to a verdict of guilt. As we have noted, the conviction was subsequently affirmed by the Supreme Court.

Sobel (1982), in a comprehensive analysis of cases involving eyewitness identification errors, indicates that counsel is especially necessary in those cases where there is not enough evidence for a formal arraignment or indictment, but a show-up or lineup is held nonetheless. The erosion of the *Wade* safeguards, beginning with Kirby, has resulted in a retreat from even the most minimal due process. The main issues at stake have been whether the identification process is reliable, whether the confrontation between the witness and the accused is suggestive, and whether other conditions could cause a distortion in memory or perception.

In a rape case, *Nell v. Biggers* (1972), the witness was attacked in a dimly lit kitchen and then taken by the attacker to an area illuminated only by moonlight, where the sexual assault took place. The defendant was convicted of rape based on a show-up and a voice identification at a police station, both of which occurred 7 months after the rape itself. The court accepted the witness's claim that she had a very good look at her assailant, indoors (which was admittedly poorly lit) and outdoors (where there was full moonlight, but no other lighting). The Supreme Court held that, despite the suggestive conditions, the identification was reliable, and it affirmed the conviction. At issue here is whether a suspect's due process rights are violated if the police are encouraged to conduct a lineup or show-up before any formal judicial proceedings, thus depriving the defendant of the right to counsel and virtually ignoring the possibility that eyewitnesses may err. One also must wonder at the weight given to an eyewitness identification and voice identification of a person the witness had seen and heard only under conditions of great trauma and poor lighting, and made so long after the criminal event. It would appear that the jury lent little credence to the scientific evidence on this crucial question.

Thus, a number of paradoxes seem to exist in a criminal justice system that has built many safeguards against wrongful conviction. A system that has created more elaborate procedures to protect defendants than any other in the world, that has given us *Powell, Miranda, Gideon, Mapp,* and *Wanderer,* has also given us *Kirby, Biggers, Ash,* and other inducements for the creation of false positives every year. Father Pagano is living testimony that, when eyewitness testimony is uncorroborated, when its shortcomings as demonstrated in scientific studies are overlooked, when it is abused by police and prosecutors, the wrong people will be identified as criminal perpetrators. The late Steve Titus is another example. How many others are there, not living but dead, either legally "dead" because they are serving long prison terms or biologically dead because they have been executed?

The problem with eyewitness testimony, as Robert Buckhout (1974) notes, is very simply stated—it is unreliable:

> Research and courtroom experience provide ample evidence that an eyewitness to a crime is being asked to be something and do something that a normal human being was not created to be or do. Human perception is sloppy and uneven, albeit remarkably effective in serving our need to create structure out of experience. In an investigation or in court, however, a witness is often asked to play the role of a kind of tape recorder on whose tape the events of the crime have left an impression. . . . Both sides, and usually the witness, too, succumb to the fallacy that everything was recorded and can be played back through questioning. (p. 23)

Almost all other experts, particularly psychologists, who have studied this question have come to similar conclusions. Along this line, A. Daniel Yarmey (1979) writes:

> The time is now ripe for an integration of psychological theories, methodologies, and findings with the law. Several areas of research interest—legal socialization, courtroom procedures, jury selection, decision processes in juries, prison behavior and prison reform, parole decisions, crime and mental illness, and so on—are currently being pursued by both psychologists and lawyers. Interdisciplinary inquiries into legal problems affecting society have begun, but only just begun. . . .
>
> Perhaps the one area in which we are most advanced and most able to make a significant contribution to the legal system is the psychology of eyewitness identification and testimony. (pp. 22-28)

The above notwithstanding, we do not want to end this discussion by leaving the impression that all eyewitness testimony is worthless, or that criminal trials could continue if there were cast over eyewitnesses a huge shadow of doubt so powerful that guilty verdicts would become even rarer, and more of the guilty would be freed.

Few important trials rest solely and exclusively on eyewitnesses, and these few are those that have created the greatest problem. Motives should be investigated (although motive is not a sine qua non in any case, and certainly not in a rape case). There is often documentary evidence to be found; blood, semen, hair, or fibers to be analyzed; alibis to be investigated and given credence, particularly when they come from excellent sources, as in the Geter case; weaponry that can be studied; and improvements that can be made in due process when eyewitness testimony is used. Many questions should be asked: What was the lineup like? Was there representation by counsel? How much trauma did the witness experience? What was the witness's distance from the suspect? How long was the witness's exposure to the perpetrator? What suggestions, if any, were made to the witness to obtain an identification?

Eyewitnesses should indeed be used, but only in the context of due process and fair trials. If due process is protected, we can have greater confidence that the guilty are being convicted, and far fewer of the innocent.

5

False Confessions,
Miranda Notwithstanding

False confessions have played a major role in the conviction of innocent people and true but illegally obtained confessions a lesser role in the conviction of guilty people. Although the police use some special techniques to obtain confessions that are true, such as confronting a suspect or arrestee with extremely incriminating evidence or with the confessions of the suspect's colleagues in crime, it is the untrue confession that is more startling. True or untrue, torture and brutality, threats, fear, and fatigue might lead to an admission, and sometimes to further information that may prove valuable to the police. Confessions have been obtained through a variety of techniques, of which the most notorious is torture, commonly known as the third degree.

Among policy makers, police, and prosecutors, use of the third degree has been justified, although seldom publicly acknowledged, when they have been certain that the person in custody was guilty, and they required a statement from him or her in order to apprehend accomplices and to obtain enough admissible evidence so that a jury would bring in a verdict

110

of guilt against a vicious perpetrator. The motivation here is to "help the jury out."

Another motivation that accounts for false confessions (and true ones as well) is the pressure on police investigators—whether from press, public, or politicians, or from within the department—to solve cases. This can lead interrogators to have a state of mind in which they are easily prone to believe in any suspect's guilt, even on the flimsiest of evidence. Once convinced of such guilt, they feel justified in resorting to any means, legal or illegal, from brutality to prevarication, from threats to promises that cannot be fulfilled, from trickery to dishonesty (including perjury), in order to prove in court what they already know, in their own minds, to be true—that the suspect committed the crime.

Although one may want to think that torture takes place only on other continents, in other countries, or that it took place only in previous centuries, this is not the case. Brutality was used, without success, in an attempt to obtain a confession from Bruno Richard Hauptmann, who was eventually convicted and executed for the kidnapping and murder of the Lindbergh baby. Not that there was any admission of this brutality; in fact, it was denied. However, there is overwhelming evidence of its occurrence in the reports of medical examinations Hauptmann received before and after the interrogation. Even though there was no confession in the case, and the brutality is irrelevant to the still-disputed question of Hauptmann's guilt, this example is relevant to an investigation of the entire question of the credibility of confessions, the conviction of innocents, and the manner in which authorities handle suspects and persons held under arrest.

The very liberal mayor of New York City in the 1930s, the beloved Fiorello La Guardia, openly exhorted the police, when they had gangsters in hand, to obtain confessions from them in any way possible, and appeared more gleeful than tearful at the prospect that blood would flow from suspects under interrogation. Although the use of brutality in the cause of obtaining admissions of guilt once had its defenders, when it is used today, at least in the United States, the fact is never openly admitted, but rather indignantly denied. Confessions made by blacks in the South were at one time both common and given little credence by those believing in fair trials and fair play. There were even coerced confessions to crimes that had never occurred. Such incidents have grown less common now, and, although racial discrimination continues to exist in the American criminal justice system, there is little evidence of the brutality that was once widely practiced, defended, and even glorified.[1]

Most confessions are not repudiated, and certainly not all repudiated confessions are made by people who are innocent of the charges brought against them. What complicates the question is that some are guilty of other charges—they are not angels—and this makes their retraction of their confessions particularly difficult and unconvincing. Nonetheless, false confessions are abundant, and once one puts aside confessions obtained through torture, physical brutality, exhaustion, and starvation, there are numerous other causes. Some people confess because certain crimes have caught the public eye; they claim guilt because of their own emotional disturbances, their need for the limelight, or the fantasies of power they create for themselves. In the 1930s, the unsolved murder of Elizabeth Short, a young and attractive California woman who came to be known as the Black Dahlia, brought forth some 2,000 confessions, many anonymous, but all of which consumed considerable amounts of the police force's time in tracking down the deliberately false leads.

Sometimes individuals make confessions to protect others, such as when an innocent man and his wife are held, and the man confesses so that his wife will be released and can go home to the children. Under such conditions, the person making an untrue admission is less concerned with the long-range than with the immediate consequences, and is apt to be confident that he or she will be able to establish his or her innocence. Others confess to minor crimes of which they are completely guiltless in order to get the matters over with, because legal fees are costly and family members and attorneys put pressure on them. They are told that a deal can be made, and they will walk away free—except for a police record. Still other individuals who are mentally retarded or of borderline intelligence may be easily led to confess or may do so to "please" interrogators.

The works of Dostoevsky contain interesting incidents of confessions. In *Crime and Punishment*, Mikolka is being held in the local jail for murdering a pawnbroker and her sister, a crime that he has admitted having committed. Porfiry Petrovich, the inspector assigned to the case, is talking with Raskolnikov, the actual murderer. What relief Raskolnikov feels when he hears of the confession, only to be told by Porfiry that, admission notwithstanding, "There is no Mikolka in it!" Raskolnikov shudders and asks who the murderer is, if it is not Mikolka: "Porfiry Petrovich recoiled, as though he could not believe his own ears. 'But it was *you,* Rodion Romanovich! You murdered them!' he went on, almost in a whisper, but his voice was full of conviction" (Dostoevsky, 1866/ 1992b).

In *The Brothers Karamazov* (18??/1992a), the question of confession and its relationship to guilt or innocence is even more complex. Three of the four brothers—all sons of the same father, the eldest from a first marriage—confess to parricide, although only one is indeed the murderer. But Dostoevsky finds built-in support for the confession in the intent and desire to kill the father on the part of those who did not carry out the killing. It is such intent, with the overwhelming feelings of guilt it can cause, that may lead to false confession. In law, however, intent without the act, and without attempts, efforts, or conspiracy to commit it, the mere thought or desire to see it carried out does not constitute legal guilt (contrary to the teachings of the New Testament, where the desire for adultery is equated with the act itself).

Psychoanalysts have, on occasion, turned their attention to the confession. It may be said that the entire psychoanalytic process, which may take place over a period of many years, constituting hundreds if not thousands of hours, is one long confessional. Theodor Reik, in *The Compulsion to Confess* (1959), reflects on the act of a patient who has admitted to something he had no intention of saying:

> The very possibility of analysis, after all, rests on the existence of just such an effective urge of those rejected impulses toward expression and their ability to assert themselves to some extent. Only through that ability of the repressed unconscious to express itself somewhere, in a distorted and displaced form, in substitute and reactive formations, have we reached a position where it is possible to recognize and interpret its signs. (p. 187)

Reik is talking here about the easing of the burden of what is in the unconscious, the cathartic effect of bringing it into the consciousness, articulating it, even if inadvertently. To our knowledge, however, no analyst, Reik or any other, has asked why people confess to crimes that they did not commit, have never had any conscious or unconscious wish to commit, and of which they usually had no knowledge whatsoever. Perhaps it is in the dark recesses of unlawful inquisitorial techniques, and not in the even darker recesses of the repressed and unconscious self, that some insights into the answer can be found.

The law has traditionally been on the side of accepting confessions, even if they are repudiated in court, and some officers of the law, inspired by police and prosecutorial zeal, anxiety to solve a case, and at times by racial prejudice, have been eager to obtain confessions by any means short of torture and brutality (and that too, although not publicly acknowledged). Courts have listened to stories of confessions by men who showed bruises, broken bones, and concussions that they did not have when taken into custody, and have heard police solemnly swear that such defendants fell down flights of stairs or knocked their heads against jail cell walls. Even more astonishing, judges have listened and have admitted these confessions as evidence, over vehement objections.

In 1964, a break in this philosophy of criminal justice came in the famous case of Danny Escobedo, who had given incriminating evidence against himself while in the custody of the police, after he had been denied access to his attorney. A sharply divided U.S. Supreme Court, by a vote of five to four, noted that "confessions have often been extorted to save law enforcement officials the trouble and effort of obtaining valid and independent evidence." The Court laid down some guidelines for the questioning of persons in custody, including the right of their families and attorneys to know where they are being held and to make contact with them, and the right of suspects to consult with their attorneys if they so request.

It was the year before the *Escobedo v. Illinois* decision (on a day that made American history because Martin Luther King, Jr., told an enormous gathering in Washington, D.C., that he had a dream) when two young women who lived in a fine section of New York City, near Park Avenue on the upper East Side, were killed in their apartment. Known as the murder of the "career girls," or the Wylie-Hoffert case (after the last names of the two victims), the slayings contained both ironies and tragedies from the beginning, and later their repercussions would have enormous effects on the interrogation process, the handing of suspects and arrestees, and the role of confessions in the adjudication of guilt or innocence (Lefkowitz & Gross, 1969).

The two victims were both white, in their early 20s, and single. Emily Hoffert was a college graduate who had come east from a small city in Minnesota, where her father was a highly regarded surgeon. In New York

City, where single people are faced with housing that is both expensive and in very short supply, many sublet and move in and out of apartments more frequently than they might like. On the day of the murders, Emily Hoffert was leaving her apartment on Eighty-Eighth Street to join a friend with whom she would share an apartment further downtown. That morning she left her home early to drive to Riverdale and obtain some luggage from another friend, brought it back to the apartment, and probably would not have stayed longer than an hour or two, just to do her packing, had her plans not been interrupted by an unexpected event.

The other victim was Janice Wylie, who had hoped for a career in the performing arts, in which she showed considerable talent, and had settled, at least temporarily, for a position at *Newsweek*. She came from a literary family: Her father, Max Wylie, was a journalist and novelist; her uncle, Philip Wylie, was a well-known novelist, essayist, and critic, a major American writer. Perhaps she would find her talent lay in the field chosen by her father and uncle.

Like Emily, Janice had not expected to be home that day, a memorable one in American history. She had planned to go to the civil rights march in Washington, and had asked Susan Brownmiller, with whom she worked, to save her a seat on the bus, so that they could travel together. Janice was not exactly an activist, but like millions of others in the United States, she had been swept into the developing consciousness of racism. But her plans, too, went awry, for she was asked to report to work that day, to be at the *Newsweek* office at about 11:00 a.m. When Emily and Janice's third roommate, Pat Tolles, went to work in the morning, Janice was just getting out of bed, and Susan Brownmiller was holding an empty seat, waiting for her friend's arrival.

Janice never arrived at work, and calls to her home went unanswered. Then people at her office, knowing her roommates and where they could be reached, called Pat, and Pat too made several calls, but without response. She thought of calling Janice's parents, who lived some four blocks from the apartment the women were sharing, but did not wish to alarm them. She decided that she would wait until she got home to see what had transpired, if anything at all.

When she arrived home, Pat found the apartment in utter disarray. She became frightened and did not wish to enter the bedrooms, instead calling the police and the Wylie family. Janice's parents arrived within a few minutes. Max Wylie entered one bedroom alone, and then emerged to tell his wife and Pat that he had found in that room the lifeless bodies of the two young women. The police arrived soon thereafter. (In one of the most remarkable and noble moments to arise out of such a gruesome tragedy, Emily's mother, notified by the Wylies by telephone of the fate of her daughter, decided that she could not call the hospital where her husband worked to pass the information on to him, because he might be needed at that moment to perform surgery.)

When this case was reported in the news media, there arose a great deal of public pressure to solve it. The murder of the "career girls" competed with the epic speech made by Dr. King for public attention and newspaper space. In addition to the simple fact that it was a double homicide, the murders became a subject of public interest because of the social class stature of the victims, the fact that the murders had occurred in an area generally considered safe (the rise in crime was not yet beginning to make itself widely felt, as it was to do in the following 30 years), the ease with which the event became known as the "career girls murder case" and by other catchy phrases, the fact that one of the victims came from a family of well-known writers, and innumerable rumors that began to spread about the lives of people whose names were found in Janice's address book.

Ironically, one of Philip Wylie's books is titled *A Generation of Vipers* (1955), a title sadly and prophetically suggesting the type of person, and the time and culture from which he arose, responsible for the death of his brother's daughter. The public clamor for the case to be broken was almost as loud as the shouts of enthusiasm, and occasional voices of denunciation, that reverberated through the land in which Dr. King had moved mountains. *Newsweek* offered a reward to any person or persons who could provide information leading to the arrest and conviction of the killer (or killers). Such rewards may not be collected by police officers or others in law enforcement, but they always have before them the greater rewards of promotions, medals, and general kudos when they break important cases—and this one was important.

Eventually, public pressure diminishes, a case is pushed off the front page, there are other worthy news stories in a world aflame and in a country beset by social problems, and there are other murders, sometimes more gory, more puzzling, more evocative of outrage. After all, only 2 months would pass before the president of the United States would be the victim of murder, an event that would monopolize newsprint and airwaves for weeks and almost months. But the assassination of John F. Kennedy only temporarily pushed the unsolved Wylie-Hoffert murders into a moment of oblivion. The pressure on the police mounted, and the reward offered by *Newsweek* was an inducement, as such rewards always are, for informers, underworld figures, and others who see an opportunity to obtain money to come up with some kind of information, even though it might be doubtful or perhaps entirely fabricated.

Many weeks went by, and although the civil rights movement gained momentum and the investigation into the Kennedy assassination aroused enormous controversy, the demand for a solution to the Wylie-Hoffert murders did not wane. Finally, there was a break in the case. The police announced that a drifter, arrested first on a charge of attempted rape and then questioned about a Brooklyn murder, had been found with a picture in his wallet—old and tattered, apparently a photo of Janice Wylie, a picture that this young, virtually uneducated, only slightly literate black youth might have obtained only if he had picked it up in the course of an event that could have started as a burglary and culminated in a double murder.

After many hours of questioning (at least 18 and possibly more than 20), without a break, the police and prosecutors emerged triumphant to face a group of journalists, microphones and television cameras in hand. They announced that George Whitmore had signed a confession to an attempted rape; to the murder of a Brooklyn woman that had occurred, virtually unnoticed, a few weeks earlier; and to the slaying of Janice Wylie and Emily Hoffert. The murder of the career girls had been solved. With confidence that did not betray the slightest glimmer of doubt, members of the Brooklyn District Attorney's Office and Brooklyn detectives announced that the right man was in custody, and there could be no question of the accuracy of that statement. Even when, a few days later, Janice's parents definitely stated that the photograph Whitmore had carried was not of her, and although that photo was the sole item that had given detectives the notion that they might have the career girls' murderer in hand, the case did not start to collapse, for one thing could not be denied—Whitmore had signed a confession.

Yes, there was a confession, and within about 2 hours after signing it, the arrested young man was in court for arraignment. He was asked if he had counsel and when he answered in the negative, he was assigned a young lawyer who just happened to be present in court that day. The two emerged from a private conference, and the lawyer announced, to the court's astonishment and to the irate denunciation of the district attorney, that his client repudiated the confession, that it was completely false from beginning to end, and that he had signed it because of mistreatment and fatigue and trickery. Eventually, everyone concerned—except for a few diehard holdouts intent on upholding the reputation of the Brooklyn law enforcement personnel—would admit that Whitmore was innocent of the crimes to which he had confessed. The name of Whitmore, as a symbol of an innocent person accused of and confessing to a capital crime, would become as well-known as the names of the victims he had not killed, and would be remembered long after they were forgotten except by friends and what would soon be left of their shattered families.

The Whitmore story has been cited in Supreme Court cases and law review articles, and entire books have been written about it. The U.S. Supreme Court mentioned it in what was to be its most famous decision on police interrogation, the *Miranda* case. One prosecutor said at a national conference that following the notorious Whitmore scandal, he lost 11 straight cases in his jurisdiction in which he had confessions—one more indication that every instance of the conviction, or even serious accusation, of an innocent hampers the conviction of the guilty. But the question remained: How did the police and prosecutors, some of them the most learned and skilled in their art in the city, with chief detectives in charge of homicide and assistant district attorneys present, obtain this false confession?

Whitmore himself claims that he was punched repeatedly, but on cross-examination he became confused as to how often he was punched, how severely, and with what effect; there was no doubt that he was not handled gently, but whether the confession resulted from physical brutality is left in confusion and contradiction by Whitmore himself. Certainly, there was more to it than that. He was exhausted, and intellectually he was no match for his interrogators. Also exhausted were the men questioning Whitmore, so they took turns, giving each other periods of rest, yet they were entirely unconcerned, or oblivious, that the youth might be even more exhausted, under infinitely greater stress, and in need of an equal or greater amount of rest. During his interrogation, Whitmore's family had come to inquire if he was being held, and they were sent away without any information, in what appeared to be a clear violation of the *Escobedo* ruling that had recently been handed down.

Among those who did not believe Whitmore's confession was Philip Wylie, who, off in Hawaii, was awakened in the morning and given some meager information about the admission and the man who had incriminated himself. Wylie scoffed, expressed his disbelief, and said that the young man was either frightened or intent on obtaining notoriety. The attempted rape and the Brooklyn murder were really small potatoes, and the Wylie-Hoffert murder had taken place in Manhattan. There, Whitmore was likewise indicted and returned to Brooklyn for trial on the attempted rape charge first, but in the office of Frank Hogan, the Manhattan district attorney, one of his youthful assistants was highly skeptical, and as he studied the case he set out to make his own investigation. He was certain that the confession related to the career girls was untrue, although he did not, in his unrelenting effort to demonstrate this, inquire as to why such an untrue confession had ever been made.

Whitmore's story does not end here. The improprieties of the Brooklyn police and of the offices of the Brooklyn and Manhattan district attorneys continued. In Manhattan, the evidence mounted that the man in custody on the other side of the East River had not committed the Park Avenue murders, but he was still being held in Brooklyn on charges equally flimsy. On the attempted rape, he was identified—under conditions that would be considered medieval within a few years—by a woman who furthermore was aware that a connection had been made with the Wylie-Hoffert case. For the Brooklyn murder, there was nothing but the confession—not the slightest corroboration. Could a confession patently false in one of its most significant components, and completely repudiated by the signer, still be admitted in court as voluntary and true in its other sections?

Furthermore, why did the police insist on prosecution after the first evidence that the confession to the Manhattan murders was false and in Manhattan there was now another prime suspect, soon to be arrested? The police may have believed that, in the prosecution of the attempted rape and of the murder of the Brooklyn woman, they would, to a small extent at least, be exonerated by the public. After all, they had nabbed an evil person, even if he was not the man they had originally, and with such fanfare, announced in blazing headlines as the slayer of the career girls.

All this led to more instances of police misconduct. It was almost as Dostoevsky contends, that crime is the cause of crime, that crime and evil cannot be contained. The woman who had identified Whitmore as the attempted rapist had torn a button from the coat he was allegedly wearing at the time (there is some question as to whether he was wearing that coat). A coat was found, and as occurs with poor people wearing hand-me-downs, several buttons were missing. The defense was never notified that the forensic laboratories of the FBI had stated that the threads did not match—those remaining on the coat were not the same as those on the button—and the assistant prosecuting attorney, who had the information from the FBI in hand, nevertheless held the button up to the jury and claimed that this button torn from this coat was proof that Whitmore was guilty and that his confession was true.

And Whitmore could not even claim that the Wylie-Hoffert part of his 62-page confession—the longest in the history of the City of New York—was admitted by the Manhattan district attorney to be false. Although by now the prime suspect in Manhattan had been arrested, and the case against Whitmore had completely collapsed, the Manhattan D.A., at the behest of his Brooklyn colleague and counterpart, did not ask for the dismissal of the indictment against Whitmore until the Brooklyn trial was over, so that the confession could be introduced without such a grave shadow hanging over it, and Whitmore, on the stand, could be identified as a man under indictment for the Manhattan murders. The repudiated confession was admitted into evidence with no indication by the prosecutors that they knew the Manhattan section of it was by now considered false.

The FBI evidence was not only withheld from the defense, but presented to the jury in a completely distorted fashion, and George Whitmore was found guilty. A day after the verdict on the attempted rape case, the Manhattan D.A. moved for the dismissal of the Wylie-Hoffert indictment, a delay for which he was denounced by the American Civil Liberties Union, the New York Bar Association, many citizens, and judicial authorities.

As for Whitmore, there would be an appeal, but before it could be made, through talks between journalists and members of the jury, it became apparent that racist remarks had been made in the jury room. The entire jury was called in and questioned, and the jurors did not deny the nature of what had allegedly transpired. In what may have been the only redeeming action taken by law enforcement personnel in this sordid affair (other than the work of Glass and some of his colleagues in Manhattan), the new district attorney in Brooklyn stated that he did not want a conviction tainted by racism, and joined with the defense in having the conviction set aside and a new trial planned. Later, Whitmore would face more trials, all an effort by authorities to salvage something from the now notorious actions of the persons who had obtained the confessions. There would be a trial on the Brooklyn murder that resulted in a hung jury, but this could not be tried a second time because by that time, because of Whitmore himself and other instances, the Supreme Court had laid down the *Miranda* warnings, to be applicable, not retroactively to all those already convicted, but to all pending cases. Without the confession, now inadmissible, there was no case whatsoever in the Brooklyn murder—not an eyewitness, not a fingerprint, not a motive, no buttons, no threads.

In Manhattan, tried for and convicted of the Wylie-Hoffert murders was a man by the name of Richard Robles, known to his friends as Rickie. He, too, confessed, but to two friends, a man and his wife, both drug dealers; the husband had recently murdered a black man, but had made a deal for the murder charge against him to be dropped if he cooperated on the Wylie-Hoffert case, in which he claimed to know the killer. (This deal prompted some to remark that the life and death of a black man had far less value to American police than the lives of whites.) Rickie Robles knew that his friend Michael Delaney had gone to the police, knew that the Delaneys' house was bugged and had seen the eavesdropping equipment, but nevertheless went to the house and talked freely about the career girls' murder. He was a man of some intelligence and showed no sign of any unconscious self-destructiveness, but his naïveté was almost beyond belief. He thought he was playing a game with the Delaneys, a game that would get his friend out of trouble, and that in the end the Delaneys would expose it for just what Robles had all along felt it was.

But the Delaneys, both heavy drug dealers, he a murderer, she a prostitute, came into court and made no hint of any game. They testified against the man who had considered them friends. Whether this type of confession—made to individuals who are not police officers but who are acting on behalf of the police—should be covered by *Miranda* has been widely debated. A little later, when Robles was arrested and the *Miranda* warnings were read to him, he insisted on talking to his lawyer. The police dragged their feet and tried very hard to convince him that it was unnecessary for him to see a lawyer; indeed, they did not notify the lawyer, who ran to the station house only when he was informed of his client's arrest by a journalist who got wind of what was occurring. After a long conference between Robles and his attorney, the lawyer left to see the district attorney.

During his attorney's absence, Robles was interrogated by some top Manhattan detectives, who later testified that he had made an oral confession. Robles, having decided not to take the stand during his trial, had no opportunity to repudiate this, and the best argument on appeal was that such interrogation was illegal, because he had already asked to see his lawyer in the case. At the time, the appeal was lost. Later, in a similar case, the court reversed itself on this issue, but it would be too late for Rickie Robles, because the new rules would not apply retroactively. We should note that we are not making any judgment here of Robles's guilt or innocence—we are only describing how the confessions were obtained.

Brutality in obtaining confessions once had its defenders, but today they are gone. The confessions of blacks in the South were at one time both frequent and given little credence, particularly after the blatant frame-up of the "Scottsboro boys." Actually none of the Scottsboro defendants ever confessed; rather, on the stand they accused others of the rapes that had not occurred, as these illiterate youths, in their fear and ignorance, unaided by counsel, surrounded by lynch mobs in a lynch court, saw this as a way of saving themselves. But this is not the same as what happened to George Whitmore. Why did he confess? Was it the brutality that he claimed, the threats, the fatigue, the demoralization, the feeling of hopelessness of the black youth surrounded by hostile whites, or was he too playing a game, having in mind that as soon as he signed his name and got into court, he would tell the truth and exonerate himself? The question we ask is broader: Why do innocents sometimes admit to crimes that can bring them extremely long prison terms, even death?

In what was for several decades the standard textbook in the field, *Criminal Interrogation and Confessions,* authors Fred Inbau and John Reid (1967) actually describe and encourage the obtaining of confessions through trickery. In this work used for training and instruction, the authors start with the premise that if a person has been arrested he or she must be guilty, and they painstakingly teach police how to obtain admissions of guilt without resorting to torture. Of the mechanisms described and most widely used, the most famous is called the "Mutt and Jeff" act (or "good cop, bad cop"), in which one detective pretends to be a very tough person, making threats, frightening a suspect, and the other pretends to be a very kind soul, interested only in the welfare of the suspect, ready to protect him or her against the severity of the colleague and the full force of the law.

Inbau and Reid's text was actually cited by the U.S. Supreme Court, in a spirit of outrage, when the famous *Miranda* decision was handed down. The Court indicated that the time had arrived to protect all prime suspects, all arrestees, from acts intended to get them to make confessions against their will, confessions that were blatantly in violation of the Fifth Amendment prohibition of involuntary self-incrimination in criminal proceedings. To convict the guilty, law enforcement personnel would just have to work harder to amass evidence; the innocent were to be protected from any repeat of what had happened to Whitmore and many others like him.

In the case of *Miranda v. Arizona* (1966), the U.S. Supreme Court took measures that some asserted would handcuff the police and others acclaimed as sure to put an end to false confessions. The consensus among criminologists today is that it did not do the former and, as for the latter, it made a contribution toward ending, but did not stamp out, false confessions. One expert, William T. Pizzi, points out that the Fifth Amendment to the Constitution states that a person shall not be compelled to be a witness against him- or herself, and argues that the Court was interpreting the word *witness* in a very broad manner, to include pretrial interrogation. Thus were born the *Miranda* warnings. In short, before suspects or arrested individuals can be interrogated, they must be warned that they have the right to remain silent and the right to have a lawyer present if they so desire, and that anything they say can be used in court against them. The *Miranda* warnings are usually read to suspects, so that they cannot later claim that parts of the warnings were omitted or given to them in different words that they did not understand.

The Bradley Cox Case

How is it possible, then, that nearly 15 years after *Miranda,* a young white male of average intelligence, to whom the warnings had indisputably been read, confessed to two heinous forcible rapes of which he was entirely innocent and that brought down upon him the incredibly draconian sentence of 50 to 200 years? Such was the fate of Bradley Charles Cox, who resided in the state of Ohio, where the crimes occurred. Cox, who has since been completely exonerated and freed, is trying to put his life together after a complete pardon following 2 despondent years in prison, during which he faced the prospect of being freed only when he was a middle-aged or old man.

Where did the criminal justice system fail in the Bradley Cox case? Why were the *Miranda* warnings insufficient? Although some of the problems may require a great deal of speculation to answer, we are fortunate in having, in this instance, a full transcript of the interrogation that led to Cox's confessions, a transcript of the trial in which the confessions were repudiated (but to no avail), information about the aftermath that established innocence beyond a reasonable doubt, and our own interview with Bradley Cox.

As in most of the cases of convicted innocents, a single cause of injustice may stand out in this case, but it is not the only cause. Bradley Cox made a false confession, after the *Miranda* warnings were read to him, and signed the confession that he knew to be false; that is primarily what concerns us at this moment. Unlike Whitmore, Cox never claimed to have been beaten, punched, tortured, or threatened with physical punishment. But even with his confession, he may still not have been convicted if there had not been several other difficulties, several strikes against him. And had some of these not existed, there would never have been a confession, and perhaps not even any interrogation or suspicion.

Cox was a Marine who had gone AWOL; he had a criminal record, and although it was for nonviolent crimes, including automobile theft, he was unlikely to be seen by any jury as an impressive and upright citizen. He had jumped bail in North Carolina, and bounty hunters were after him. Having spent time in a North Carolina jail, his dread of being returned there or sent to a navy brig made him an easy mark for interrogators who, sometimes by subtle hint and sometimes with outright statements, promised him a better fate if he confessed. He was poorly educated, a high school dropout, and was gullible. He believed in people who talked nicely to him, who treated him kindly, who said that they had only his best interests in mind.

The crimes had been committed several months before Cox's arrest, and his alibis were hesitant, uncertain, unverifiable, and self-contradictory, on the one hand casting doubt on his credibility, and on the other adding to the growing suspicion of the police officers who had him in custody that he might be the guilty person, after all. His attorney was a public defender who was overworked and had little time even for a case that was going to result in what could be longer than a lifetime sentence, working within a budget that was inadequate to conduct the independent investigation necessary to determine whether there was exculpating evidence.

From the transcript of the case, it is clear that Cox's attorney did a competent but by no means brilliant job. There was at least one opportunity for the attorney to call for a mistrial that he missed completely—not unusual in the heat of battle and when one must recognize the opportunity within a few seconds, but something that might not have occurred with a large staff and a sharper, more quick-witted, and no doubt more expensive attorney—or battery of attorneys—sitting at the defense table.

Working against Bradley Cox was another factor: The enormity of the crimes, the particular cruelty of the rapes, committed in a rather quiet area of Lancaster, Ohio, had aroused not only fear but public indignation, creating an atmosphere where the pressure on the police to solve the crimes was enormous. In such circumstances, a detective with a suspect in hand is more easily led to believe that the suspect is indeed guilty and that arrest, trial, and conviction will lead not only to public safety, but to public acclaim for the detective as a hero, with accompanying possibilities of promotion.

The two rapes, and a third one that was eventually charged to Cox (but for which he was never tried, although the police listed it as cleared by arrest) had similar modus operandi and were committed within a reasonable distance of where Cox lived. If he had committed one, as the police and eventually a jury came to believe, then there was little doubt that he had done the second, and probably the third. Also, after his arrest (in fact, several weeks before it), the rapes had come to an end, and no one suspected (for there was no reason to suspect it) that a serial rapist, passing through Ohio, had raped these three women. This rapist would continue on his criminal rampage in Oklahoma, Texas, Louisiana, and elsewhere, his modus operandi essentially unchanged. Even after Cox's arrest and conviction, interstate exchange of criminal information was too scanty and haphazard for this to come to light, and Ohio officials breathed easier, for they believed the rapist was now behind bars and the attacks on women by this man, particularly cruel attacks, had ceased.

Yet, in the end, with all of these facts, some admissible in a court of law and others not, there was nothing but the confession. The rapist had always worn a ski mask, so that although the victims and their husbands, in both the Lancaster cases, had had a good look at him, they said in court that they could not identify Cox, and that they had no knowledge of ever seeing him before. There was some weak evidence that Cox had borrowed a car the night one of the crimes was committed, the car in which the criminal drove to the scene, but the witness who testified about this became tangled in the usual type of cross-examination. When asked how he remembered that night, what was so different about it, he said that he could recall so well because that was the night his friend Brad had committed the rape!

The parade of witnesses for the prosecution described the crimes in detail: the brutality, the pain, the humiliating features, the type of evidence that victims and their proponents believe should be allowed to be aired in a courtroom (particularly when the woman has the willingness to state such painful and humiliating events in public). To stop such testimony on the grounds of irrelevance, because the facts of the crimes and the manner in which they had been committed were not in contention, but only the culpability of the man on trial, would have been prejudicial to the jury. One might, however, have argued that the testimony was irrelevant to the issues at hand, and hence their repugnant details could only prejudice jurors on the question of whether Bradley Cox was the perpetrator and could only divert attention from this sole issue and toward the question of the enormity of the events.

The case came down to the confession, repudiated in court, as had Whitmore's been a few years earlier, but given for different reasons and under different circumstances. And it brought into question whether even *Miranda* is adequate to protect an innocent suspect, particularly given the finding of guilt and the sentencing of Cox to 50 to 200 years. And if not *Miranda,* what can be done?

Let us look back on the Cox story from the vantage point of what was not known at that time to anyone but Bradley Cox and a wandering serial rapist who was hundreds if not thousands of miles away, and perhaps did not even know that someone was under arrest for crimes he had committed—namely, that Cox was innocent. Cox's immediate family, his parents and an aunt living nearby, may have believed him (and one would like to think that his attorney believed him, although guilty people have protested their innocence to attorneys so often that one cannot entirely blame counsel if belief in the guiltlessness of this client was less than certain). Knowing, as we do now, that Cox was innocent; that there is no charge or evidence that torture or brutality was used against him; that the

Miranda warnings were read to him, not once but at least twice; and that Cox was an adult (certainly, the idea of reading *Miranda* warnings to a child who is to be questioned has an absurdity to it), we can look at the transcripts to attempt to discover the source of the injustice.

There are two sets of transcripts, the first of the interrogation itself, and the second of the trial. The main focus should be on the first, to determine what occurred that led to the confession. And why, when Cox had strongly recanted that confession, was a jury willing to bring in a verdict declaring that Cox had indeed committed the rapes, and that this had been proved beyond a reasonable doubt? We are interested not only in how false confessions are obtained, but in how they lead to false convictions. We shall also focus on futile efforts to repudiate false confessions.

Between the Whitmore and the Cox confessions, both now conceded by all parties to be false, there are some major differences. Most important are the *Miranda* warnings, which came into existence in the period intervening between the two cases, partly in fact due to the Whitmore interrogation. Yet the *Miranda* warnings did not work to save Cox. Both confessions were repudiated almost immediately, Whitmore's, in fact, within minutes after his arrival in court. Whitmore claimed that he had been punched, pushed, and kicked during interrogation; Cox made no such claims. Both men were made promises. Whitmore, who was very young, legally blind, almost illiterate, and demoralized, who had been sleeping in doorways, was promised some assistance in improving his situation. Cox was promised that he would be treated with far more kindness than he would receive if he were sent back to North Carolina. Both were subjected to the common police interrogation technique known as the Mutt and Jeff act.

That Whitmore was black and accused of killing two white women as well as a black woman (in a far less publicized case) did not help. There are many indications that he was a victim of racism, in the jury room without any doubt, and possibly also in his treatment by detectives. Both Cox and Whitmore may have been provided information during interrogation that, innocent as they turned out to be, they could not have known; yet the denials of the interrogators that any such information was fed to them are on the record.

For criminal justice, the two cases had entirely different aftermaths. Cox, after 2 years in prison, was exonerated and released. His case attracted only slight interest outside of Ohio. Whitmore's case achieved national notoriety, not only because the murders were already famous, but because his repudiation of the confession, and its rejection by higher judicial and prosecutorial authorities, cast the New York Police Department, its high-ranked detectives on the homicide squad, and the office of the Brooklyn District Attorney in an incredibly malevolent light. Whitmore continued to be prosecuted (one might almost say persecuted) for a number of other crimes, particularly an attempted rape and the Brooklyn murder; further rulings by judges cast shadows on the integrity of the criminal justice system.

The rapes for which Cox was convicted were solved by another arrest, of Jon Simonis, the "ski mask rapist," who had been traveling up and down the country and, it turned out, had passed through Lancaster, Ohio. The guilt of this second man for the crimes of which Cox had been convicted was conceded by everyone, including the interrogator who had been the chief defender of the false confession and who traveled to Louisiana to interview the newly arrested Simonis. By contrast, in Whitmore's case it was the New York District Attorney's Office that had doubts, as did many others, including Philip Wylie, who pointed out the unbelievable nature of Whitmore's statement the very day of the arrest. The district attorney then indicted a second man, Richard Robles, who was indeed found guilty and sentenced to a long prison term. Finally, in what may have been an unprecedented event in the history of criminal trials, the defense in the Robles case called as a witness one of the chief detectives who had gotten the confession from Whitmore, and the New York County district attorney, in cross-examining the detective, characterized him as a liar (although he used words much more pejorative than that).

The primary investigator in the Whitmore case was Joseph DiPrima. During the interrogation, DiPrima had been asking Whitmore where he had obtained a photograph found in his possession that seemed to the detectives (although, as it turned out, they were mistaken) to resemble Janice Wylie. Another detective, Edward Bulger, was in the room, and Whitmore was frightened of Bulger. The prisoner said he had stolen the photo from a house he had been in, in New Jersey, where he had lived and where his parents were then living. What happened next? According to Bulger and DiPrima, the following exchange occurred at this point in the interrogation:

Bulger Are you sure you stole it from that house, or didn't you steal it someplace else?

Whitmore Someplace else.

Bulger Where?

Whitmore I stole it from an apartment house.

Bulger Where? Where?

Whitmore From an apartment house in New York.

Bulger Where? Where? What street?

Whitmore Eighty-Eighth Street.

DiPrima Thank you, George.

Eighty-Eighth Street—they had hit pay dirt, or so they claimed. But George Whitmore tells the story of this segment of an interrogation that would go on for some 20 hours as having occurred in a different manner:

> Mr. DiPrima kept on askin' me where did I get the picture from, so I told him I found it, figurin' he would stop askin' me the questions, so he said, "Couldin' you have got this picture off Eighty-Eighth Street?" I told him, "I have never been on Eighty-Eighth Street in my life." And he called me a liar.
>
> He kept insistin' that I got this picture off Eighty-Eighth Street. I told him I never been on Eighty-Eighth Street, so he said, "Dint you go to Eighty-Eighth Street and go into an apartment and take this picture?"
>
> I told him no, no, I never been there before. But he kept on askin' me questions over and over and over. An' so I told him yes. "Yes, I got them there. Eighty-Eighth Street."

And so it was with all the other information that went into the long confession. What a wealth of details George Whitmore knew! And then the 62-page statement was read back to him. After all, he had 20/200 sight, making him legally blind, and without his glasses, which he was constantly losing or breaking (and did not have with him at the station house), he could not read it himself, although he managed to sign his name. Whether every word was read to him is doubtful, but he admitted, out of fatigue and weariness and a sense of helplessness and fear, and out of a belief that these people would help him, that he had broken into an apartment and hurt two girls. He claimed to have been told that the girls were recuperating in a hospital, and that they had forgiven him for what he had done. Knowing that he was being forgiven for what he had not done, he did not find this to be a difficult way out of his dilemma. It was the next morning, only a few hours later, in fact, that he discovered that the girls had been killed and that everyone now "knew" that he was the killer.

The same kind of use of suggestion was repeated in the case of Bradley Cox. In the early part of February, Cox was arrested for rapes that had occurred the previous August and October. As in Whitmore's case, there were two elements to the interrogation that led to Cox's confession: promises of help (we will help you, you need help, we will protect you) and the feeding of information to the suspect so that he could give it back. Cox was on drugs and in trouble elsewhere, and promises of help appear constantly throughout the transcripts of his interrogations. Here are a few examples from his interrogation by Detective Don Regan:

Regan Do you understand we want to get you help?
Cox Yes, sir.
Regan And the only way we can help you is if you are truthful. Have you told anybody about this incident?
Cox No, sir.
Regan OK, are you aware that this is being recorded?
Cox Yes, sir.
Regan And you have talked to us, have we promised you anything or pressured you or anything?
Cox No, sir.
Regan Are you giving this of your own free will? Do you want help?
Cox Yes, sir.

After he is asked if he will sign the statement and answers in the affirmative, the exchange goes on:

Regan Is there anything else you want to add to this, Brad?
Cox I just appreciate the help I'm being given by you and other than that—that's it.

The case against Cox came down to the confession. He was not identified by any of the victims. The evidence given by one of his buddies had an aura of doubt—why did the young man remember what was happening this particular day, when he admitted that one day was like another? That Cox was far from an upright citizen at the time was true, but he was a youth with no record of violence. He was more than confused with his alibis, and he had undoubtedly lied and improvised at various points, but that could have been out of fear; it was hardly enough to convict a person. There were no fingerprints, not a single piece of forensic evidence, no semen tests, and no unusual behavior before or after the events on Cox's part to tie him to the crimes.

On April 25, 1980, Bradley Cox took the witness stand, told how he had joined the Marines, how he had rented a car that he did not return and was apprehended and sent back to North Carolina, where, after a weekend, he was placed in a civilian jail in Jacksonville. On direct examination, Cox said about the jail:

All the people in there was black sheep, the Marines that got thrown in there. I couldn't tell you if it was day or night. I didn't—if I had a lawyer, I didn't even know of it. I had to fight for my food day in and day out, which didn't amount to anything. . . . The people that was in there was crazy. More or less, they were nuts. I couldn't—I couldn't rest. I could sleep, but I couldn't rest at all. Continuous harassment and fighting all the time. No communications with anybody, except when I got to call my aunt, and I only got to talk for two minutes.

After 3 months, he was released from jail on a bond for which he was able to put up $200. He made his way back to his Marine unit, and when he got another paycheck, he again went AWOL, catching a plane for Columbus, and then from there had gone to Lancaster. A bondsman had put up the money to get him out of jail. On direction examination, in an effort to repudiate the confession, his lawyer elicited the following exchange:

Q Do you know what the bondsman would do to you [if you were caught upon failure to return to court]?

A Yes.

Q For not showing up when you were supposed to?

A Oh, yeah. They told me.

Q What did they tell you?

A They'd shoot me. They would just as soon—they would rather take me back in their trunk than in the back seat and have to feed me. And I had to sign papers saying that was okay, you know.

Cox met Detective Regan while he was in Lancaster; the first meeting was probably on January 31, 1980. "He approached me as a friend," the defendant stated, on the stand.

Q Did you discuss your life and your problems with him?

A Yes.

Q Did you discuss your problems in North Carolina?

A Yes.

Q Did you indicate your fears and distaste for North Carolina?

A Yes.

Q Did you indicate a desire to have him help you?

A Yes.

Q Did he offer his assistance to you?

A Yes.

Q How was this assistance offered, in what form?

A Well, he just came on to me as though North Carolina wouldn't be able to get hold of me, he'd make sure of it personally.

Regan treated him in a friendly manner, he went on to explain, got him food, chicken dinners, soda pop, cigarettes. For an entire week, Regan mentioned one of the rapes, and for the entire week, Cox denied any knowledge of or involvement in it. The detective, and his associate, Lieutenant Hopkins, had made certain statements (by their own admission and as shown in the pretrial interrogation transcript) that there was a possibility that Cox could be charged only with robbery and not with rape. It was at this point, Cox testified, that he opened up, played their game. A robbery charge, with all the friendly help that he would get from Regan, did not sound too bad; the alternative was virtual kidnapping by a bounty hunter working for the bail bondsman and being taken back to the hated jail in North Carolina (or the Marine brig), this time on a further charge of being a fugitive from justice and AWOL. The direct examination continued:

> Q What was the gist of what they said about North Carolina?
> A "If you want to cooperate with us"—this was Detective Regan—"if you want to cooperate with us, then I can help you."
> Q And what did "help" to you mean?
> A Mean "help" him?
> Q What did "help" to you, by him mean?
> A Keep me out of North Carolina.
> Q Did he make that clear to you?
> A Yes.

And so Cox went along with their story, seduced by the friendly attitude of the detective. The promises, according to the defendant, were clear:

> He promised me if I cooperated with him that he wouldn't—he wouldn't charge me with the rape. He would just charge me with the robberies. He also gave me a little bit of time [not time to think of a response, but meaning that Cox would have to serve time for the robbery]. I'd get time. He'd promise me time at Lima, halfway house, nut house; whatever.

As for the prospect of being returned to North Carolina: "He promised me that they wouldn't be able to touch me. They wouldn't be able to take me down there."

How did Cox get to know so much about the events that took place in the homes where the crimes occurred if he had not been the perpetrator, and if he had never been in those homes and did not know the people? Cox claimed that, during a week of interrogation, Regan fed him answers, gave him data as to what had happened: "He came right out and told me [about the ripping of the towel]. He told me that—that that's what happened in plain words." And in other instances, "the questions that he asked me had the answer tucked right in them." Cox sought to please. "If you don't cooperate and give me the answer, then I can't help you," he quoted the detective as having said to him. When the answers had not worked out he would make up new ones. Furthermore, there had been a great deal of talk about the two rapes in the town, and through gossip and rumor many details become common knowledge; not everything was as secret as one might be led to expect by reading an assistant district attorney's charge that only the criminal could have known these things.

In fact, when the chips were down, there was only one statement that could not be traced to common knowledge, to information being fed by the detectives, to stumbling from one answer to another until the correct one was hit upon, or to an answer "tucked into" a question, as Cox put it. This was a matter of identifying a lubricant, which the rapist had evidently made an effort to use. What lubricant was it? Cox had been asked, and after his usual hesitation, his desire to please, he mentioned Vaseline. Correct the first time. No one had told him it was Vaseline, and the prosecutor was going to make the most of it. He had not guessed wrong, had not been asked the question two or three times until he came up with the correct answer that would please the friendly detective who was out to help him. How could he have chosen Vaseline, of all the lubricants on the market, the cross-examining attorney would demand of him, if he had not been in the house and if he were not the rapist? "It just came into my mind, the one I thought of," he would answer, and it is only now, knowing that he was telling the truth (a truth conceded by Regan as well as the prosecutor), that one finds this believable. But, after all, it is not far-fetched—the word Vaseline is almost synonymous with lubricant, as Xerox is with duplicating machine, although it is a trade name. What would have come to anyone's mind trying to please an interrogator by finding a trade name for a lubricant—KY? Noxzema?

For other questions, there had to be repetitions, the questions asked several times, "every which way so I can understand what he was getting at, so that I could answer them the way he wanted me to." And, with one case under his belt, the detective came back a few days later and told the prisoner that there was still another case, and that he would need his cooperation if that was going to be solved, too. Again, the same denials, then admissions, inability to give details, statements that Cox made, about himself later, that he could not remember some things because he was on drugs.

To impeach Cox's testimony, to uphold the integrity of the detectives, to obtain a conviction, the prosecutor found many discrepancies in the defendant's account of the days when he had talked to Regan. These were not minute matters, because these were the days when he was allegedly being fed the information that would appear in the confession. There was discussion as to why he had originally been apprehended by Regan, and Cox gave a simple answer: There was pressure not only on himself, but on his family, including his aunt; he was tired of running and hiding.

> It was brought out to me by my people that—it wasn't more or less said straight out. They was trying to keep it quiet. But I could see—I had—somehow I had known that Regan was making my people believe that he could help me. And in turn, their concern was since they had a detective, a low [*sic*] officer, that he had to be honest saying, "Yes. I will help your son get out of this mess and get back on the right foot," that they believed.

The following excerpt of the transcript of prosecutor Holt's cross-examination of Cox is an interesting colloquy that throws light on the criminal justice system and the anxiety, or at least overzealousness, on the part of some law enforcement authorities to have heinous crimes solved. The reader should examine this in light of the knowledge that the defendant was innocent and had confessed nonetheless.

Q Do you know why Detective Regan would want to apprehend you, rather than the real rapist?

Mr. Williams [counsel for defense] Object, Your Honor. Asking for mere speculation.

The Court No. He asked if he knows why. He can say yes or no.

Mr. Holt I asked him, do you know.

A I believe in my own personal belief that through people I have known, and heard about and seen, that when you go to work day after day after day for months on end, and you got a man down on top of you every day about finding this man, if you nab the rapist, you nab the rapist; if you don't you don't. He wanted it off his shoulders. He seen me. He found a prime suspect that he could pick off.

Q So he didn't care whether you did it or not?

A That's my belief.

Q He didn't care that there was a rapist who did the things that those women testified to running around in this community? You are telling me he didn't care about that?

A I am not saying he don't.

Q If you are not the man, and if he doesn't care about which man he's got, isn't that exactly the situation that's going to be existing in this community?

A That's right, because the person who did it is still running around, because I ain't him.

In his summation, Williams stated, perhaps partly for the purpose of not antagonizing a jury with a frontal attack on a police officer, what might be a key:

I think Detective Regan had all the good intentions of the world. But I am not up here trying to tell you that he was lying or anything of the sort. I know the Defendant thinks he was, because he's bitter about this thing, after having been taken advantage of, promised things. But I think Detective Regan thought these things were done, and in his eagerness he questioned, and questioned, and questioned the Defendant until he had talked about just about everything about his case during the week a little bit.

And later, Williams discussed the deal that Cox thought he had made:

Think about Lieutenant Hopkins of the Ohio State Patrol, and think about his testimony that he did remember an arrangement where Brad would plead to robbery, and the other things would be forgotten. He testified there was an arrangement. He testified he made the statement that that's not a bad deal. He didn't dream that up.

In rebuttal, Holt put the matter very bluntly:

But when it really comes down, you have to say, "Is Detective Regan lying? Is he, or is the Defendant?" Because if Detective Regan is not lying, there can be no question, no question for common sense and reason, that Mr. Cox committed these crimes.

These must be difficult words for Holt to read today; Bradley Cox must find them difficult as well, as must Detective Regan.

It was 5:25 p.m. on April 25, 1980, when the jury retired after hearing the charge. At 8:45 p.m. the jury announced that it had not reached a verdict, and deliberations were recessed until the following morning. The next day was a Saturday; all morning there was deliberation in the jury room, but without a verdict, and by lunchtime there was another recess. After lunch, the jury returned, and came in with its verdict at 3:30. The verdict was guilty on all counts, and when the defendant came up for sentencing, whatever might have been left of Detective Regan's promises had disappeared. Cox was sentenced to 50 to 200 years in prison.

Two years later, Bradley Cox was exonerated. Although the false confession was almost the sole piece of evidence against him in the original trial, one can find a number of other explanations for his conviction, and for his making the confession in the first place: Cox's criminal record; his fear of apprehension by bounty hunters working for the bail bondsman; his dread of being returned to another state where he had suffered in the jail and prison system; extreme overzealousness on the part of detectives and prosecutors; community pressure to stop a series of extremely heinous crimes; his own extraordinary naïveté; and a public defender who was undoubtedly competent, but who had few or no investigative funds and a heavy caseload, who missed at least one opportunity for a mistrial (when Cox was characterized as the man who had just committed a rape by a witness testifying as to his whereabouts the night of one of the crimes), and who perhaps treated Regan and Hopkins a little gently in cross-examination in light of what the transcript clearly shows were promises and misrepresentations that had been improperly made to Cox. With all that said, however, it comes down to the fact that Cox did make a confession and the *Miranda* warnings did not prevent him from doing so. If *Miranda* is insufficient to protect the innocent, where can one turn?

Most confessions are no doubt true and reasonably accurate, Whitmore and Cox notwithstanding. But the importance of confessions for solving cases, and for building solid cases for trial, has been exaggerated. Many jurists have noted that confessions are often used by law enforcement personnel as excuses to avoid time-consuming investigatory work, and that, when repudiated, confessions have little value if this other work has not been accomplished. *Miranda* was meant to give protection to all those held in custody, but evidently it failed in Cox's case. By a curious quirk, although *Miranda* was not in effect at the time of Whitmore's confession, the decision saved Whitmore as well, because it applied to all pending cases when it was handed down, and there was still hanging over Whitmore the possibility of a new trial for the Brooklyn murder. With the *Miranda* ruling, which came about in part because of the scandal over Whitmore's confession, and with the Brooklyn murder consisting of no evidence except the now inadmissible confession, Whitmore was spared another trial for a crime of which he was undoubtedly both ignorant and innocent.

Some have suggested that any confession repudiated in court should be barred. If the confession will not be made in the presence of the attorney (as the *Miranda* court had intended except when the defendant was so positive of his abilities as not to request a lawyer), then a court retraction vitiates the intention of *Miranda*. This would actually affect very few cases, for most confessions are followed by pleas of guilty. The problem with leaving the credibility of a repudiated confession up to a jury, it is said, is found in the injustice inherent in a system in which rich and poor, able and unable defendants, families, and lawyers do not compete on a level playing field.

Against a poor defendant who must rely on a court-appointed attorney who is underpaid, overworked, and possessed of few funds and little or no investigatory staff (although sometimes extremely dedicated and extraordinarily effective) are all the forces of the prosecution, with government funds, detectives, police, and a confession to parade before a jury. By contrast, wealthy defendants are not only very unlikely to confess without their attorneys present, but if they do so, they can employ batteries of lawyers for which the prosecution is no match. This is not to say that the rich have never gone to prison; they have, not only for white-collar crimes, but sometimes for murder and other violent crimes, not to mention drug dealing.

Even *Miranda* can sometimes fail, and it did in the Robles case. Robles insisted on seeing his attorney, and after many delays and efforts to dissuade him, and after his attorney was notified by a journalist rather than by the police that he was being held, he did confer. But then the attorney left Robles to spend about half an hour with the district attorney, only to return to find that three top detectives had come to the cell in the meantime and had obtained what they claimed to be an oral, unsigned confession from the prisoner. The detectives so testified in court, and for reasons unrelated in all probability to the confessions, Robles did not take the stand. The right of the defendant not to take the stand is well integrated into American criminal trial procedure, and this right, the jury is warned, is not to be interpreted as concealing guilt; there may be many other reasons, including particularly a prison record that will be disclosed on cross-examination, but will not be known to the jury otherwise.

Without taking the stand, Robles could not repudiate the confessions, so they stood, unchallenged, unrebutted, *Miranda* warnings notwithstanding. On appeal, this question was raised but rejected by the higher court; since then, in New York State, the courts have ruled that once an attorney has entered a case, the prisoner may not be interrogated by police or prosecutors without the presence or specific permission of the attorney.

A more radical and far-reaching proposal has been made recently that would eliminate entirely police and prosecutorial interrogation of a prime suspect or a prisoner, but at the same time would retain the prisoner's right to refuse to testify as a witness on the grounds of possible self-incrimination. The Constitution is sacred to Americans, as is the Bill of Rights, and although many have felt that the Fifth Amendment has been abused, there is little clamor for its repeal, and even less likelihood of it. Under the proposed system, before a magistrate, with prosecution and defense lawyers present, an accused would have to answer questions, account for his or her whereabouts, tell what he or she knows about a crime. This proposal, put forward in the United States particularly by Lloyd Weinreb, a prestigious professor of criminal law, is in effect an attack on the adversary system. It suggests nothing less than the first steps toward the Continental (or inquisitorial) system of justice, turning the courts into areas of inquiry into matters of dispute, where trained personnel are at hand to protect society and individual members, and from which truth and justice must emerge.

False confessions today play a rather minor role—at least quantitatively—in our study of convicted innocents. They can be diminished by better police training, with emphasis on investigators' duty to uncover truth and not to further their careers (and jeopardize public safety) by breaking big cases at whatever cost; by more careful scrutiny of details and discrepancies by prosecutorial officials, as was done by the young assistant district attorney in Manhattan who first read the Whitmore confession and set out on an investigation to disprove what was admitted therein; by consideration of motives or conditions that might lead to a confession (promises, low IQ, interest in protecting another, youthful naïveté); and by a general rule that confessions, when repudiated and without corroboration, are insufficient to warrant convictions.

As for the principal characters we have discussed in this chapter, we know the following. George Whitmore was the victim not only of racial prejudice, but of harassment on the rape charge, in which the prosecution depended not only on the false conviction but also on evidence of a button allegedly torn from his coat by the victim. Prosecutors presented this evidence in court without informing the defense or even the court and jury that the FBI laboratory evidence was more damaging to the prosecution's case than it was to the defense. After the first trial was thrown out because of racial prejudice, Whitmore was tried again, and the judge ruled that the false confession, insofar as it related to Wylie-Hoffert, could not be introduced by the defense in order to impeach the entire confession. At that point, the defense stood mute, refused to enter an affirmative defense, and Whitmore was found guilty. In court he spoke, almost eloquently, against his attorney, and said that he had been deprived of his day in court. He was tried for the Brooklyn murder, and there was a hung jury, leaning almost completely for a verdict of not guilty. He was released on bail, but then was remanded to prison after the guilty verdict on attempted rape and then received a third trial, in which he was exonerated. He was never awarded any compensation for his false arrest, conviction, and imprisonment. George Whitmore has since fallen into obscurity.

Rickie Robles was found guilty of the Wylie-Hoffert murders. The fate of an ex-convict, particularly someone convicted of violent and still-remembered murders, is difficult to predict. The appeal in his case was based entirely on a technicality, not on the weight of the evidence. Some writers have expressed the belief that Robles was not guilty, but that, after Whitmore, a scapegoat had to be found for the Wylie-Hoffert murders; they hint that the murderer was an Englishman who knew Janice Wylie, acted very strangely after her death, and then returned to England and disappeared from sight. The case against Robles was strong, however. More interesting than speculation about another murderer is the remark made by Philip Wylie: Were the means used to arrest and convict Robles justified, even if he is guilty?

Bradley Cox is free; he has married, and he is still adjusting to the upheaval his arrest and conviction caused in his life. The tricked confessions and the extraordinary sentences he received, the prospect that he faced for 2 years that he would be spending all of his life in prison, left deep emotional marks upon him, as did his treatment at the hands of the other prisoners, who regarded him as a rapist. Rapists, along with child molesters, are among the most detested of all prisoners, and one can only imagine the impact such treatment can have. Our interview with Cox confirmed this point.

As for those who did wrong in these cases, among the police and prosecutorial teams, there were many, not only in the interrogations, but in the suppression and distortion of evidence and in the failure of the Manhattan district attorney to drop the indictment against Whitmore in order to please his buddy across the river. Some were censured, but the dishonor rolled off their shoulders and they continued their careers, unfazed by the events in which they had a hand. Many of the detectives hurriedly retired, some were demoted temporarily, others were even promoted. No one was dismissed for improprieties, and no one was indicted for perjury, not even some Brooklyn detectives who, in the Robles trial, were denounced by the prosecution as liars and perjurers. All of this is, sadly, commonplace in such cases of injustice. Even where law enforcement officers and prosecutors have been proved to have engaged knowingly in deceit and unethical conduct leading to false convictions, they have rarely received more than a reprimand. From the perspective of deterrence theory, this is a clear-cut situation where there are too few disincentives to deter this kind of behavior, absent professional ethics.

Note

1. This historic shift has not been of a linear nature in all nations. Amnesty International continues to document the torture of suspects, many of them innocent, in many nations of the world. Aleksandr Solzhenitsyn (1973), in discussing the former Soviet system of "justice," summarizes the use of torture as follows: "It is more accurate to say that before 1938 some kind of formal documentation was required as a preliminary to torture . . . then in the years 1937-1938 . . . interrogators were allowed to use violence and torture on an unlimited basis, at their own discretion. . . . In 1939 such indiscriminate authorization was withdrawn, and once again written permission was required for torture. . . . Then, from the end of the war and throughout the postwar years, certain categories of prisoners were established by decree for whom a broad range of torture was automatically permitted" (p. 99).

6

Wrongful Conviction and Public Policy

What Can Be Done?

The inspector . . . turning to the prisoner, "What do you demand?" said he.
"That . . . if innocent, I may be set at liberty."
"When were you arrested?" asked the inspector.
"The 28th of February, 1815, at half-past two in the afternoon."
"To-day is the 30th of June, 1816; why, it is but seventeen months."
"Only seventeen months!" replied Dantes; "oh, you do not know what is seventeen months in prison!—seventeen ages rather, especially to a man who, like me, had arrived at the summit of his ambition—to a man who, like me, was on the point of marrying a woman he adored, who saw an honourable career open before him, and who loses all in an instant, who sees his prospects destroyed, and is ignorant of the fate of his affianced wife, and whether his aged father be still living! Seventeen months' captivity . . . is a worse punishment than human crime ever merited."

Alexandre Dumas, The Count of Monte Cristo, 1846

The sense of injustice and moral indignation associated with wrongful imprisonment is powerfully conveyed by Dumas in his classic *The Count of Monte Cristo*. Like most of the subjects of our research,

Edmond Dantes found himself unjustly deprived of liberty and thrust into a frightening world behind walls—in his case, without even having had the benefit of a trial.

Unlike Dantes, real-life modern-day prisoners cannot emerge from prison and, transformed into the Count of Monte Cristo, exact their retribution. Unlike Dantes, most of those whose cases we have examined were not the victims of conspiratorial witnesses. Instead, most of our subjects were falsely convicted because of unintentional errors made by witnesses and by those who staff and operate the justice machine in the United States—the police, prosecutors, defense attorneys, and judges.

Of course, not all of these errors were unintentional. Not all of them were products of innocent, careless mistakes. The ugliest and most unsettling incidents uncovered by our research involved outright lying, the fabrication and alteration of evidence, the intimidation and coaching of witnesses, and perjury and the suborning of perjury. Why? Convinced of a suspect's/defendant's guilt, police and prosecutors simply want to make certain that he or she will not "get off" or "beat the rap." If that requires a little deceit, then isn't it for a good cause? Doesn't the end justify the means?

Does it? Are the citizens of the United States so frightened of crime that we are prepared to tolerate intentional violations of suspects' or defendants' rights in order to "get them off the streets"? Do we believe that the court decisions protecting suspects' and defendants' rights have gone too far, and that police and prosecutors must engage in some unethical and unprofessional conduct in order to restore the balance between good and evil—to reinforce that "thin blue line" that protects us from the uncivilized elements of our society? Or, in condoning such behavior—even if it were to lead to some marginal benefits in deterring crime—would we not have a "cure" that is worse than the "disease"? Would we not, in defeating the enemy, have become our own worst enemy? These and other public policy questions surround the issue of wrongful conviction.

Crime Control Versus Due Process

Mankind censure injustice fearing that they may be the victims of it, and not because they shrink from committing it.

Plato, *The Republic,* 3rd century B.C.

It is not within the realm of possibility to prevent all wrongful convictions. A system of law that never caught an innocent person in its web would probably be so ineffectual that it would catch few of the guilty as well. Herbert Packer's classic work *The Limits of the Criminal Sanction* (1968) provides a useful theoretical framework for analyzing wrongful conviction and public policy in the United States. Packer's "crime control" and "due process" models, though theoretical constructs, are useful in assessing the relative emphases of particular aspects of the criminal justice process. Not surprisingly, those aspects of our criminal justice system that emphasize crime control objectives (plea bargaining, for example) may not only help control crime but also contribute to system error and wrongful conviction.

Moreover, our research has established the existence of an important systemic phenomenon that has significant implications for the production of false convictions. We call this phenomenon the *ratification of error.* That is, the criminal justice system, starting with the police investigation of an alleged crime and culminating in the appellate courts, tends to ratify errors made at lower levels in the system. The further a case progresses in the system, the less chance there is that an error will be discovered and corrected, unless it involves a basic issue of constitutional rights and due process.

To use Packer's (1968) distinction, the criminal justice system can tolerate factual errors, but not legal errors. Although one might argue that eyewitness misidentifications and false accusations, for example, are factual errors, the legal error lies in the system's failure to discover what is occurring and stop the course of events before a wrongful conviction occurs. A previously noted case illustrates this point, as well as the interactive character of the errors leading to most wrongful convictions.

Recall the case of Nathaniel Carter, who was falsely convicted of stabbing his ex-wife's foster mother. A *New York Times* analysis of police reports, court records, and more than 100 interviews reveals a succession of serious errors, neglect, and outright incompetence that collectively led to Carter's wrongful conviction:

1. An officer and another witness saw a man in bloody clothes running from the murder scene—a man whose description did not match Carter's. In violation of prescribed practices, however, their accounts were never passed on to the prosecutors or the defense attorney, and the incident remains unexplained.

2. A prosecutor lied at the trial, leading the jury to believe that Carter had admitted he was at the crime scene on the day of the murder.

3. The district attorney's staff never questioned Carter's ex-wife's story, despite her background of violence. Instead, shortly after receiving the case, the district attorney granted her immunity from prosecution.

4. The defense attorney failed to contact many of the witnesses who saw Carter far from the scene of the murder at the time it was committed. Of at least 10 such witnesses, only 2 were ever called to testify ("How Errors Convicted," 1984).

As one observer commented, "This was a breakdown of major proportions in the justice system. . . . It is a justice system so overworked that it has grown cynical to the possibility of a man's innocence." Carter characterized his experience more succinctly: "I was railroaded" ("How Errors Convicted," 1984).

The Carter case illustrates one of the major findings of our study—that in most cases of wrongful conviction the system breaks down in more than one way. This is at once both reassuring and alarming. It is reassuring that one error made by one individual seldom results in wrongful conviction; it is alarming that sometimes many errors can occur in one case, as in Carter's.

What, as a matter of public policy, can be done about wrongful conviction? We believe that our study has implications for prevention, identification and exoneration, and compensation. In examining the public policy implications of our study, we shall address three major questions:

1. What is the meaning of wrongful conviction for our society and its criminal justice system?
2. How can the number of wrongful convictions be reduced?
3. What can be done for those who are wrongfully convicted?

In considering these questions in the context of our study, we shall also offer policy proposals designed to address these issues. We will restrict our proposals to those we regard as both justified and practicable, avoiding others that, though theoretically interesting, seem to us highly impractical.

What Is the
Meaning of Wrongful Conviction?

Injustice anywhere is a threat to justice everywhere.
Dr. Martin Luther King, Jr., 1963

The very essence of our society is freedom and all its existential, social, economic, and political implications. Therefore, there can be no more important issue than the deprivation of freedom and under what conditions such deprivation should be permitted to occur. Next to execution, imprisonment is the single greatest power the state has over its citizens. In our view, imprisonment should, therefore, be used sparingly—as a "last resort" form of social defense against those who have demonstrated that they pose a risk to public safety and cannot be controlled in the community.

"PRISON-FLATION" AND ITS MEANING FOR A DEMOCRACY

Our current overreliance on prisons (about one million citizens are imprisoned at any one time, and the incarceration rate in the United States is by far the highest of any free society) constitutes a type of inflation. In economic inflation, the value of each monetary unit is cheapened because there are so many units. In "prison-flation," the societal meaning of imprisonment (and the human lives involved) is cheapened by its massive overuse. Winston Churchill recognized this during his brief term as home secretary in 1910-1911, when he observed that the overuse of imprisonment posed a threat to free societies, and he set a determined course to restrict England's reliance on prisons. As a result, imprisonment in England was reduced during a period of rising crime (Rutherford, 1984).

- **Policy Proposal 1:** The current reliance on imprisonment should be significantly reduced.

A sharp reduction in the use of imprisonment would have many advantages, but for the purpose of our study the most important would be the restoration of significant meaning to the act of imprisonment. Just as "body counts" on the evening news desensitized Americans to the meaning of individual deaths in the Vietnam War, the national "prisoner counts" issued regularly by the government report such staggering numbers as to render us insensitive to the meaning of imprisonment—a severe intrusion by the government into the lives of its citizens. Reducing the number of citizens who are imprisoned will focus more attention on those who do receive this sanction and will help to ensure that the evidence solidly warrants such a drastic means of social control. Many nonviolent prisoners can be adequately punished in community-based correctional programs, which can even include house arrest and electronic monitoring. Such increased scrutiny of our reliance on prisons should help reduce the incidence of wrongful conviction and imprisonment in our society.

LOSS OF CONFIDENCE
IN THE CRIMINAL JUSTICE SYSTEM

The classical period in criminology (1800-1876) was dominated by the utilitarians, such as Jeremy Bentham, and their vision of "rational man." Deterrence theory is predicated on those rationalist views. Perhaps the most recognizable symbol of justice in our society is Justicia, or "Lady Justice," with her scales. But when the scales tilt too far in the direction of deterrence and crime control, due process rights suffer. And when the public learns that innocent persons have been convicted and imprisoned, it may lose confidence in the justice system and in the law as an institution. This may then have a number of dysfunctional implications, one of which could be that it will become increasingly difficult to secure convictions owing to the public's (and jurors') cynicism toward the police, prosecutors, and other representatives of the government.

As the reader will recall, such a crisis occurred in the spring of 1985 in the state of Illinois when a man convicted of rape, Gary Dotson, had his prison sentence commuted after the alleged victim, Cathleen Crowell Webb, recanted her testimony. This complex case received intense public and official scrutiny, including public hearings conducted by Governor James Thompson, a former law professor and prosecutor. The case elicited considerable public criticism of and cynicism toward the criminal justice system. Interviews with other alleged rape victims who were preparing to testify in their own cases at the time revealed these women's belief that the Dotson/Webb case would make it much more difficult for juries to believe their own testimony. Likewise, when a series of errors occurs as in the Carter case, mentioned above, can anyone doubt that this increases public cynicism concerning "evidence" and "proof"?

Or consider the Florida cases of James Richardson and Todd Neely and the impression they might have had on citizens, and potential jurors, in the state of Florida. Though Richardson's life was affected for a much longer period than Neely's, both injustices illustrate important "system dynamics" that must be understood and, to the extent possible, addressed.

Richardson, a poor black farmworker from rural Florida with an IQ of 77, was convicted of poisoning seven of his own children and stepchildren by lacing their lunches with a pesticide. He was imprisoned and sentenced to death in 1968 and served nearly 22 years before being freed and declared the victim of a tragic frame-up, just one month after Randall Adams was released in Texas. The prosecution had argued that Richardson had killed the children to collect on their life insurance, which, they claimed, he had purchased the night before the murders.

Actually, what was portrayed as evidence that he had purchased insurance was merely an insurance salesman's business card. Further, the babysitter who had cared for the children, and who later was diagnosed with Alzheimer's disease, had admitted to her nurses "more than 100 times" that she had in fact killed the children. And finally, a former cell mate, who had testified that Richardson had made a jailhouse confession, later stated that he had been beaten and coerced into lying by a sheriff's deputy. Richardson's appellate attorney, Ellis Rubin of Miami, was quoted in the *New York Times* as saying of the case, "The name Richardson is destined to become equated with prosecutorial misconduct." Like Randall Adams, Richardson narrowly escaped execution during his ordeal.

Todd Neely, an 18-year-old boy living in Martin County, Florida, with his parents, was yet another victim of the system. Neely was at dinner with his parents on the evening of June 17, 1986 (and had a time-stamped receipt to prove it) at the time a young woman 11 miles away called 911 and reported that she had been attacked by a boy who was "16 max" and wore braces on his teeth. Neely had an alibi and did not fit the victim's description of the assailant, whereas a 14-year-old boy in the same neighborhood did fit the description, had a history of exhibitionism and voyeurism in the neighborhood, and, as it turned out, had told friends he had committed the crime. Nonetheless, Neely was arrested and charged with attempted first-degree murder.

Circuit Judge C. Pfeiffer Trowbridge, a 29-year veteran, heard the case without a jury. The defense opted for a nonjury trial and the prosecution

agreed to allow Professor Elizabeth Loftus to testify concerning identification factors (such testimony is usually not permitted in Florida). Observers felt that Judge Trowbridge treated Loftus disrespectfully and
seemed to imply that he might have resented the use of such an "expert"
in the trial. The judge found Neely guilty and sentenced him to 15 years
in prison.

But Neely, like Randall Adams, had a strong and determined family.
Lew and Edith Crosley, Neely's parents, devoted their time, energy, and
financial resources to proving Neely's innocence. Finally, a year after a
motion for a new trial had been denied, the Florida Department of Law
Enforcement was asked by the state's attorney general to review the case.
On August 24, 1989, all charges against Neely were dropped. One of the
key rationales for this decision was the court's conclusion that key
exculpatory evidence had been withheld from the defense ("How the
Wrong Man," 1990). Neely's wrongful conviction cost his parents nearly
$300,000 in legal expenses and untold emotional trauma and personal
anguish. They recovered only about half of their monetary losses in a
subsequent award from the state—although they fared better than the
victims of similar injustices in Texas, who have never received any
payments from that state. Although Neely spent "only" 92 days in jail, his
experiences in this case were not exactly compatible with the develop-
mental needs of 18-year-olds. Needless to say, the case elicited a great
deal of public sympathy and cynicism—at least temporarily.

Finally, occasional instances of police brutality—even torture of suspects to extract confessions—come to light and, though certainly infrequent, further undermine public confidence in law enforcement and the
administration of justice. In May 1985, for example, four New York City
police officers from the 106th Precinct House in Queens were arrested
after being accused of extracting confessions from suspects by jolting
them with an electronic stun gun. An examination of one of the victims
revealed 40 burn marks on his body. Mayor Koch called for a ban on the
newly issued stun guns, the entire top command of the precinct was
transferred, and the police commander for Queens retired from the force.
This incident is just one among many that have recently undermined
confidence in New York City's police—some 81 New York police officers
were arrested for crimes in 1984, and 22 more in the first quarter of 1985
(as reported in the May 6, 1985, issue of *Newsweek*).

- **Policy Proposal 2:** There is an inverse relationship between the number of wrongful convictions and confidence in the criminal justice system. Therefore, reducing the number of wrongful convictions will increase confidence in the criminal justice system and may actually increase the conviction rate.

WRONGFUL CONVICTION AND PUBLIC SAFETY

In our discussions of this study and the general subject of wrongful conviction, we have observed that, for some reason, "liberals" seem to be more concerned about this problem than are "conservatives." This is somewhat peculiar, for two reasons:

1. Wrongful conviction is frequently attributable, at least in part, to violations of constitutional rights—an issue that has historically concerned conservatives.
2. For every case of wrongful conviction, the actual offender remains free, perhaps to victimize additional citizens.

For these reasons, we believe that wrongful conviction should be an issue of concern to all citizens, whether liberal, moderate, or conservative; Democrat, Republican, or independent; political, apolitical, or anarchist.

- **Policy Proposal 3:** There is a need for public education on the subject of wrongful conviction and its dysfunctional implications for our society.

Reducing the
Incidence of Wrongful Conviction

As we have noted, our study suggests that eyewitness misidentification is the factor most often associated with wrongful conviction. There exists a substantial body of evidence demonstrating that eyewitness identification is an unreliable source of evidence under any circumstances. The emotional trauma associated with criminal victimization casts even further doubt on the accuracy of human perception and memory.

What are the implications of this finding? Should we preclude eye-witness testimony? Hardly—to do so could lead to the acquittal of many guilty persons. What, then, can be done to balance the need for such testimony with the problem of its tenuous reliability?

- **Policy Proposal 4:** In cases where eyewitness identification is the sole evidence and there is no corroborating evidence, a jury or a judge should hear, in a special pretrial session, all information related to the issue and should decide the adequacy, validity, and reliability of the eyewitness identification in each case.
- **Policy Proposal 5:** In cases where eyewitness identification is in-volved, the court should always permit the use of qualified expert witnesses and should issue precise cautionary instructions to juries.
- **Policy Proposal 6:** When a crime occurs, law enforcement authorities should make a special effort to conduct investigations of all eyewit-nesses and victims as soon as possible, in order to minimize the consequences of memory distortion.
- **Policy Proposal 7:** No identification procedure (pre- or postin-dictment) should be conducted in the absence of the defendant's attorney.

Following eyewitness misidentification, the next most important con-tributing factors are law enforcement and prosecutorial errors and misconduct. Our study suggests that unintentional errors far outnumber intentional misconduct.

Although it may be impossible to eliminate unintentional errors com-pletely, we make the following suggestion:

- **Policy Proposal 8:** The basic and advanced training of law enforce-ment personnel, prosecutors and their staffs, and judges should in-clude consideration of wrongful conviction, including its causes, its implications for our society and for the criminal justice system, and methods of prevention. This training should include the presentation of detailed case studies of wrongful conviction, focusing on witness errors, police and prosecutorial errors, official misconduct, and judi-cial failure to detect errors at trial and on appeal.

As we have indicated, most of the errors made by police and prosecutors, as well as judges, are unintentional. Better training can reduce, but not eliminate, such errors. Further, we are not concerned here with cases in which law enforcement officers and prosecutors, acting in good faith, arrest and prosecute someone who is eventually found not guilty, because no violation of public trust has occurred in such cases. We are, however, very concerned with those instances of intentional conduct of an unethical and unprofessional nature. Our research has convinced us that such conduct in the United States has not, in general, received appropriate attention, nor has it been adequately punished. In a number of nations, such conduct would simply not be tolerated and would cause great political scandal if it occurred. Therefore, as a deterrent to such conduct, we propose the following:

- **Policy Proposal 9:** Law enforcement officials or prosecutors who (a) knowingly alter, conceal, fabricate, or otherwise distort evidence; (b) commit perjury; (c) intimidate or bias witnesses or suggest information to them in order to strengthen cases against defendants; (d) knowingly enter into plea bargain agreements in bad faith, ignoring the existence of potentially exculpatory or mitigating evidence; or (e) fail to make available to the defense in a timely manner (especially after discovery motions) all information or evidence of a potentially exculpatory or mitigating nature should be removed from their positions of public trust and subjected to the most severe civil, professional, and (where appropriate) criminal penalties. For prosecutors, this should include disbarment proceedings, because such misconduct, if proved, is a clear violation of public trust. Likewise, law enforcement personnel who commit such acts should be permanently removed from their positions, because such behavior is incompatible with public confidence in the police.
- **Policy Proposal 10:** To assist in implementing the above proposal, state and local bar associations, prosecutors, and state attorneys general should routinely evaluate the performance of law enforcement officers and prosecutors involved in every case of known wrongful conviction, as such cases occur. Also, judicial performance in such cases should be reviewed by the appropriate body in each state (for example, the state supreme court). Such reviews will serve to

provide evidence of any actions requiring sanction and will provide the basis for continuing education concerning such cases.

Identifying and Exonerating Convicted Innocents

In Packer's (1968) discussion of the due process model, he notes its emphasis on "quality control." To achieve that goal, the due process model incorporates certain assumptions about postconviction appeals:

1. The trial process represents a forum in which official abuses of power often occur; therefore, appellate review represents both a safeguard for the individual accused and an opportunity to elaborate upon the rights of the individual.
2. There should be no limitations on the right to appeal; the inability to afford filing fees, transcripts, attorneys, and so on must not stand in the way of an appeal.
3. The decision concerning bail pending appeal must not be manipulated so as to discourage appeal and ought to be made by the appellate court rather than by the court of original jurisdiction.
4. The appellate court should be entitled to consider any error prejudicial to the rights of the accused.
5. There should be no single standard for determining what constitutes reversible error.
6. Any error that violates the defendant's basic rights should be grounds for reversal, independent of the strength of the case against the defendant.
7. Abuses that occur at the trial level, such as prosecutorial misconduct, prejudicial publicity, and ineffective counsel, must be sanctioned at the appellate level by reversing the conviction of the defendant (Packer, 1968, pp. 230-232).

Having examined hundreds of cases of wrongful conviction, we believe that Packer's prescriptions remain important safeguards. Often-expressed concerns about the numbers of "frivolous" postconviction appeals are understandable with respect to court management; however, with respect to justice, we firmly believe that new trials should be granted where reasonable concern about errors exists, and that postconviction appeals for justice "by reason of innocence" should be permitted, as should postconviction appeals on the basis of prejudicial error. It is only through the liberal use of postconviction remedies that our courts can demonstrate their continuing concern with possible error and their intention to extend citizens' rights past the prison gates. Such continuing concern may have prevented the 24 years of wrongful imprisonment endured by Isidore Zimmerman; the 21 years James Richardson spent in prison for poisoning his own children; Randall Adams's 12½ years in prison, including 3½ years on death row, for killing a police officer he had never seen; Steve Titus's ordeal, which probably cost him his life, even though his death did not occur in confinement; or the execution of accused Lindbergh baby kidnapper Bruno Richard Hauptmann, who, whether guilty or not, was subjected to a highly prejudicial trial, including a grossly incompetent performance by defense counsel.

INADEQUATE COUNSEL

Unfortunately, being inadequately represented by defense counsel is a problem that goes far beyond the celebrated case of Bruno Richard Hauptmann, whose lawyer seemed so thoroughly intimidated by the public stature of Colonel Lindbergh that one wonders whose side he was on. The investigating authorities, who initially found two sets of footprints outside the Lindbergh home, were permitted to testify as if Hauptmann acted alone. Colonel Lindbergh was allowed to claim, under oath, that a distant voice he heard in a dark cemetery was unmistakably that of Hauptmann. Such highly objectionable testimony went unchallenged by Hauptmann's defense attorney. If one were searching for a classic case of inadequate counsel that should serve as an embarrassment to our adversarial system of justice, this one would have to rank very highly.

Another controversial case involving a sham trial served to provide the basis for an appeal of a conviction on the basis of inadequate counsel. In *Powell v. Alabama* (1932), Ozzie Powell, one of the "Scottsboro boys," did have some representation, but, like Hauptmann's, it was most inadequate for a capital case. The basic rationale for such an appeal is that the original defense counsel, for whatever reasons, did not adequately represent the client's interests in the case. Such appeals are not easy to win, despite the fact that many attorneys are inadequately prepared for trial work.

Even more threatening to our legal system are the "cop-out lawyers" who make comfortable livings by pleading defendants guilty without investigating the cases or even interviewing the defendants. Silberman (1980) points out that such "wholesalers" may charge a mere $50 per case, but by averaging five pleas a day (not difficult when no investigation or interview is conducted), they can earn well over $50,000 a year. One Los Angeles attorney is apparently so good at this that he can enter as many as 25 guilty pleas a day at $200 each. Even the highest-paid corporate attorneys cannot match his $5,000 per day income.

- **Policy Proposal 11:** State and local bar associations, as well as state and local public defender commissions, should routinely evaluate the performance of defense attorneys involved in known cases of wrongful conviction, as such cases occur. Such reviews of attorney performance will provide evidence that may be used in invoking professional sanctions, if warranted. Moreover, such inquiries will provide information on attorney performance that will be useful in continuing legal education programs and in law school curricula and clinical programs. Where resources permit, a random sample of criminal cases should be examined to assess the adequacy of defense counsel, whether appointed or privately retained. Such random assessments should serve to provide some quality control in the delivery of legal services to defendants, thus reducing the number of wrongful convictions.

Compensating and Reintegrating Convicted Innocents

In our growing concern with the crime problem, our society has begun to embrace some of the ideas of Margaret Fry, the noted British magistrate and social reformer who should be viewed as "the mother of crime victim compensation." Fry advanced the argument that the government, as well as the offender, has a responsibility for compensating the crime victim. She reasoned that government has a duty to protect its citizens from violent crime and, failing that, must then at least indemnify them. Her proposal for a government-sponsored social insurance program for crime victims has now been widely adopted throughout the United States and in many other nations (Newton, 1976).

Such programs to compensate crime victims and to provide them with the services needed to make them whole again make sense. They also help restore respect for the justice system and the institution of law in our society. Crime victims are often embittered both by their initial victimization and by their subsequent treatment by the criminal justice system. Victim compensation and victim aid programs help restore their respect for the criminal justice system and for the society in which they live.

Should we not be equally committed to compensating and reintegrating the victims of our criminal justice system—the wrongfully convicted and their families, who have suffered unjustly? Despite the compelling claim such individuals have, the fact is that their treatment has been a national disgrace. After discovering what we have done to them, we have in most cases given them very little financial compensation and almost no assistance in reintegrating themselves into society. Rosen (1976) noted that the United States has lagged far behind many nations in its failure to compensate the innocent victims of erroneous criminal accusations.

The fact is that in most states, in order to compensate a citizen who has been convicted but is later found to be innocent, a special bill must be introduced and passed by the state legislature. Such a bill generally empowers the state court of claims to set the amount of the award, and claims courts tend to apply very conservative criteria, such as the amount of lost wages and the legal expenses incurred by the wrongfully convicted individual. Given the economic status of most wrongfully convicted persons, the use of criteria such as "lost wages" cannot begin to approximate the cost of time spent in prison as a result of false conviction.

Only a handful of states (California, Wisconsin, Illinois, New York, and Tennessee) have established special funds for compensating the victims of wrongful conviction. Even in these states, however, the awards are generally small; in some cases, the statutorily prescribed ceilings on such awards amount to $5,000 or less per year of imprisonment (American Bar Association, 1984). The other option for these individuals seeking compensation, of course, is through civil litigation, but this can be impractical. One attorney, whose client was awarded only $5,800 by the Wisconsin

Claims Board after serving 14 months in prison for an armed robbery he didn't commit, commented:

> You're talking about an expensive proposition. My client certainly doesn't have the money to pursue a civil suit. Most of these cases aren't like [Lenell] Geter. They're not getting the publicity. These are small cases in comparison and these people have to take what they can get. Sometimes they don't get anything. (American Bar Association, 1984, pp. 34-35)

We believe that states should acknowledge their responsibility to provide fair compensation for innocent citizens who have been wrongfully convicted, or at least for those who have been wrongfully incarcerated. As Ohio's Tenth District Court of Appeals proclaimed in reversing a "grossly inadequate" Ohio Court of Claims award that "shocked the conscience" of the appellate court:

> No society has developed a perfect system of criminal justice in which no person is ever treated unfairly. The American system of justice has developed a myriad of safeguards to prevent the type of miscarriage to which the claimant herein was subjected, but it, too, has its imperfections. Fortunately, cases in which courts have unlawfully or erroneously taken a person's freedom by finding him or her guilty of a crime which he or she did not commit are infrequent. But, when such a case is identified the legislature and the legal system have a responsibility to admit the mistake and diligently attempt to make the person as whole as is possible where the person has been deprived of his freedom and forced to live with criminals. Indeed the legal system is capable of creating few errors that have a greater impact upon an individual than to incarcerate him when he has committed no crime. (*O'Neil v. Ohio*, 1984)

The following year, the state of Ohio's Court of Claims awarded William Bernard Jackson (known in the Ohio media as "the wrong Jackson") a total of $717,500 for the 5 years he spent in prison for two rapes he did not commit. This judgment consisted of $67,500 for loss of earnings, $200,000 for loss of liberty and separation from family and friends, $200,000 for injuries and adjustment problems in prison,

$100,000 for damage to Jackson's reputation, and $150,000 for legal fees. The award was subject to income tax on the $67,500 paid for lost wages, but the remainder of the award was tax-free, according to the Internal Revenue Service. In addition, the Ohio Court of Claims stated that it expected to pay Jackson $3,000 in interest from the date of the award to the date of issuance of the check.

This compensation and two awards of $1 million each (one of which was reduced on appeal) are among the largest judgments for wrongful imprisonment in U.S. history. Although such cases attract widespread publicity, typical awards have been very small, often amounting to pennies for each hour spent in prison, rather than the $16.54 per hour received by William Jackson.

Although it is unlikely that legislation enacted in states will be so broad as to encompass all wrongfully convicted persons, we believe that an important step could be taken in enacting statutes to compensate and reintegrate into society those who are wrongfully incarcerated. Therefore, based on our research and our familiarity with many such cases, we make the following proposal.

- **Policy Proposal 12:** State legislatures should enact statutes for the financial compensation and socioeconomic reintegration of wrongfully convicted persons. Such statutes should include at least the following:

  1. loss of liberty and separation from family and friends;
  2. physical injuries, mental anguish or humiliation, or other adjustment difficulties while incarcerated;
  3. all actual and unreimbursed expenses and costs incurred in legal defense, including attorney fees and court costs;
  4. damage to reputation;
  5. any other damages directly related to incarceration;
  6. either actual lost wages (based on average income earned during the 3 years prior to incarceration) or median family income, based on aggregate state statistics, for each year of wrongful incarceration, whichever is greater; and
  7. the services (at no cost) of state-supported employment agencies and other social service agencies whose assistance may be useful in reintegrating the wrongfully incarcerated citizen.

Because of the media attention and political sensitivity surrounding controversial cases, many state officials are extremely reluctant to be put in the position of "retrying" such cases, a position that has many political liabilities and few, if any, advantages. Therefore, some state legislatures may wish to enact statutes that provide for the *automatic* compensation of wrongfully incarcerated citizens, along guidelines such as those proposed above or some other "formula," rather than insisting that such persons obtain the sponsorship of a legislator through a special "enabling" bill. To date, perhaps the best such statutes are operative in New York and Ohio, though they are not without implementation problems.

The Ohio compensation statute also created a universe of cases that were analyzed as part of a recent study by Ishiyama, Desai, and Huff (1993). This analysis of wrongful convictions in the files of the Ohio Court of Claims (which administers Ohio's compensation program for the wrongfully convicted) indicates that the same factors discussed throughout this volume were involved in the first 14 cases coming to the Court of Claims for compensation. The researchers identify four types of bias that commonly appeared in the wrongful convictions analyzed: case biases (e.g., forensic evidence, witness identification, past record of the accused), societal biases (e.g., community pressure, racial/ethnic/political stereotypes), process biases (e.g., adversarial system, "stacking" in favor of prosecution), and structural biases (e.g., crowded court dockets, cost of defense, lack of police resources).

Ishiyama et al. (1993) suggest that in addition to an accuser, a common feature of wrongful convictions is a role they call the "process vigilante" (often a law enforcement officer or prosecutor) who actively constructs and nurtures case biases, views societal biases as tools to invoke in reweighting the process of justice, views structural biases as opportunities to build on, and views process biases as the principal threat to be blocked. The existence of such process vigilantes represents a threat to our system of justice and underscores the urgent need for policy reform.

Although wrongful conviction can never be eliminated in a system involving human judgment, we are convinced that it can be greatly reduced through a focus on *preventable errors*. We owe it to those victims of the system whose cases we have presented in this book—and to those who, though innocent, will be convicted tomorrow—to make such errors rare.

One of the authors has argued in previous work that one of the best ways to understand the dynamics of our own criminal justice system is to analyze it in cross-cultural perspective (Huff, 1987). We need much more cross-cultural research to address such questions as which systems are most effective in meeting their crime control mission while at the same time generating few errors. Is ours really the best system in the world, as is often claimed? Also, what differences exist in societal tolerance for this type of injustice and why? Is such tolerance for injustice related to the perceived or real magnitude of the crime problem in the society?

Capital Punishment:
The Irreversible Error

The final issue we wish to address concerns the ultimate power of the state—to deprive a citizen not only of liberty, but also of life. Based on our own research, as well as that of Radelet and Bedau (1992), we believe that the possibility of human error, intentional or unintentional, must be taken more seriously by policy makers. The pages of this book, as well as Radelet and Bedau's extensive listing of wrongful convictions in capital or potentially capital cases, document the fact that many individuals have faced death knowing that they were innocent. Not all of them were executed, mercifully, but some were and others could have been. Some have come within hours of death.

Convictions in the United States are supposed to be based on proof of guilt "beyond a reasonable doubt." This is not the same as proof beyond *any* doubt, nor do we believe that such a perfect standard would be attainable. However, in recognition of the fact that conviction can occur without ruling out all doubt, we believe that our sentencing policies should, in addition to other rationales, take this fact into account. Therefore, given that convictions are based on a probability of guilt rather than a certainty of guilt, all convictions ought to be reversible and the corresponding punishments compensable if it is discovered that errors have been made. And all of them are (in the sense that the falsely convicted person can be freed and compensated), with one exception: capital punishment. What can be done when we discover that we have executed an innocent person? Compensate his or her estate? Apologize to the deceased's family? If, on the other hand, the individual is serving a life term in prison, we can at least release him or her and make financial compensation through a reasonable formula (though it could never be adequate) for the loss of freedom and for lost wages, legal expenses, and other related costs.

We believe that the majority of the public (even in the United States, where capital punishment is widely supported) would support this policy shift if it were to include the option of life imprisonment either without parole or with eligibility for parole set only when the prisoner has reached advanced age, for those offenders convicted of first-degree murder or equally heinous crimes. This shift in policy would also accommodate the concerns of a substantial number of people whose support for the death penalty erodes as soon as the wording of the survey question introduces the possibility of error.

- **Policy Proposal 13:** In recognition of the possibility of error, the death penalty should be abolished in favor of life sentences for those convicted of first-degree murder or other equally heinous crimes. This would enable the state to release and compensate the wrongfully convicted upon discovery of error. States not willing to implement this policy recommendation fully should give consideration to a policy of "partial abolition"—that is, the death penalty should never be imposed in cases relying on witness testimony and circumstantial evidence and lacking compelling physical and other corroborating evidence.

References

Adams, R. D., with Hoffer, W., & Hoffer, M. M. (1991). *Adams v. Texas.* New York: St. Martin's.

Adams, R. D. (1993, May 19). *Adams versus Texas.* Lecture presented as part of the Walter Reckless Memorial Lecture Series, Ohio State University, Columbus.

Allport, G. W., & Postman, L. J. (1974). *The psychology of rumor.* New York: Henry Holt.

American Bar Association. (1984, June). Innocents in jail. *American Bar Association Journal, 70,* 34-35.

The bad and good luck of Lenell Geter. (1984, March 8). *New York Times,* p. 14.

Bedau, H. A., & Radelet, M. L. (1987). Miscarriages of justice in potentially capital cases. *Stanford Law Review, 40,* 21-179.

Borchard, E. M. (1932). *Convicting the innocent: Sixty-five actual errors of criminal justice.* Garden City, NY: Doubleday.

Brandon, R., & Davies, C. (1973). *Wrongful imprisonment: Mistaken convictions and their consequences.* London: Allen & Unwin.

Bredin, J. (1986). *The affair: The case of Alfred Dreyfus.* New York: George Braziller.

Brennan, W. J. (1961). *The Bill of Rights and the states.* Santa Barbara, CA: Center for the Study of Democratic Institutions.

Brigham, J. C. (1981). The accuracy of eyewitness evidence: How do attorneys see it? *Florida Bar Journal, 55,* 714-772.

Brigham, J. C., & Barkowitz, P. (1978). Do they all look alike? The effects of race, sex, experience, and attitudes on the ability to recognize faces. *Journal of Applied Psychology, 8,* 306-318.

Brigham, J. C., & Malpass, R. S. (1985). The role of experience and contact in the recognition of faces of own- and other-race. *Journal of Social Issues, 41,* 139-145.

Brislin, R. W. (Ed.). (1990). *Applied cross-cultural psychology.* Newbury Park, CA: Sage.

Brown, E., Defenbacker, K., & Sturgill, W. (1977). Memory for faces and the circumstances of encounters. *Journal of Applied Psychology, 62,* 311-318.

Buckhout, R. (1974). Eyewitness testimony. *Scientific American, 231,* 23-31.

Buckhout, R., Figueroa, D., & Hoff, E. (1975). Eyewitness identification: Effects of suggestion and bias in identification from photographs. *Bulletin of Psychonomic Society, 6,* 71-74.

Buckhout, R., & Greenwald, M. (1980). Witness psychology. In J. Imwinkelreid (Ed.), *Handbook of forensic evidence.* New York: Practicing Law Institute.

Carter, D. T. (1969). *Scottsboro: A tragedy of the American South.* Baton Rouge: Louisiana State University Press.

Chance, J., Goldstein, A. G., & McBride, L. (1978). Differential experience and recognition memory for faces. *Journal of Social Psychology, 97,* 243-253.

Chapman, G. (1955). *The Dreyfus case: A reassessment.* New York: Reynal.

Clifford, B. R., & Scott, J. (1978). Individual and situational factors in eyewitness testimony. *Journal of Applied Psychology, 63,* 352-354.

Court stand-in is convicted of crime he didn't commit. (1980, July 17). *Atlanta Constitution,* p. 12A.

Crime and punishment in Dallas. (1989, July). *ABA Journal,* pp. 52-56.

Cross, J. F., Cross, J., & Daley, J. (1971). Sex, race, age, and beauty as factors in recognition of faces. *Perception and Psychophysics, 10,* 393-396.

Crowder, R. F. (1976). *Principles of learning and memory.* Hillsdale, NJ: Lawrence Erlbaum.

Davies, G., Shepherd, J., & Hadyn, E. (1979). Effects of interpolated mugshot exposure on accuracy of eyewitness identification. *Journal of Applied Psychology, 64,* 232-237.

Dershowitz, A. M. (1983). *The best defense.* New York: Random House.

Dinnerstein, L. (1968). *The Leo Frank case.* New York: Columbia University Press.

Dostoevsky, F. (1992a). *The brothers Karamazov.* New York: Macmillan. (Original work published 1821)

Dostoevsky, F. (1992b). *Crime and punishment.* New York: Macmillan. (Original work published 1866)

Ehrmann, S. (1962, March). For whom the chair waits. *Federal Probation,* pp. 14-25.

Ellison, K. W., & Buckhout, R. (1981). *Psychology and criminal justice.* New York: Harper & Row.

Feingold, G. A. (1914). The influence of environment on identification of persons and things. *Journal of Criminal Law, Criminology, and Police Science, 5,* 39-51.

Finer, J. J. (1973). Ineffective assistance of counsel. *Cornell Law Review, 58,* 1077-1120.

Fishman, G., Rattner, A., & Weimann, G. (1987). The effect of ethnicity on crime attribution. *Criminology, 25,* 507-524.

Frank, J., & Frank, B. (1957). *Not guilty.* Garden City, NY: Doubleday.

Freed Jackson's advice for wrongfully accused is to get venue change. (1982, September 25). *Columbus Citizen-Journal.*

Gardner, E. S. (1952). *The court of last resort.* New York: William Sloane.

Going, M., & Read, J. D. (1974). Effects of uniqueness, sex of subjects, and sex of photograph on facial recognition. *Perceptual and Motor Skills, 39,* 109-116.

Granelli, J. S. (1980, December 15). Trials—and errors. *National Law Journal,* p. 1.

Gregory, W. L., Mowen, J. C., & Linder, D. E. (1978). Social psychology and plea bargaining: Applications, methodology and theory. *Journal of Personality and Social Psychology, 36,* 1521-1530.

Henshel, R. L., & Silverman, R. A. (1975). Introduction. In R. L. Henshel & R. A. Silverman (Eds.), *Perception in criminology.* New York: Columbia University Press.

How errors convicted the wrong man. (1984, March 15). *New York Times,* p. B1.

How the wrong man almost went to prison. (1990, December 31). *Miami Herald,* pp. 1A, 10A.

Huff, C. R. (1987). Wrongful convictions: Societal tolerance of injustice. In J. L. Miller & M. Lewis (Eds.), *Research in social problems and public policy* (pp. 99-115). Greenwich, CT: JAI.

Huff, C. R., Rattner, A., & Sagarin, E. (1986). Guilty until proved innocent: Wrongful conviction and public policy. *Crime & Delinquency, 32,* 518-544.

Inbau, F. E., & Reid, J. E. (1967). *Criminal interrogation and confessions.* Baltimore: Williams & Wilkins.

Innocent prisoner gets $1 million. (1980, September 4). *San Francisco Chronicle,* p. 38.

Ishiyama, H. J., Desai, A., & Huff, C. R. (1993). *Wrongful conviction in Ohio: Rights and roles.* Unpublished manuscript.

Isidore Zimmerman, 66, man unjustly jailed for a murder. (1983, October 14). *New York Times,* p. 25.

Kalven, H., & Zeisel, H. (1966). *The American jury.* Boston: Little, Brown.

Kennedy, L. (1985a). *The airman and the carpenter: The Lindbergh kidnapping and the framing of Richard Hauptmann.* New York: Viking.

Kennedy, L. (1985b). *Ten Rillington Place.* New York: Avon. (Original work published 1961)

Laughery, K. R., Alexander, J. E., & Lane, A. B. (1971). Recognition of human faces: Effects of target exposure time, target position, pose position, and type of photograph. *Journal of Applied Psychology, 55,* 477-483.

Lavrakas, P. J., & Bickman, L. (1975). *What makes a good witness?* Paper presented at the annual meeting of the American Psychological Association, Chicago.

Lefkowitz, B., & Gross, K. (1969). *The victims: The Wylie-Hoffert murder case and its strange aftermath.* New York: Putnam.

Leippe, M. R., Weil, G. L., & Ostrom, T. M. (1978). Crime seriousness as a determinant of accuracy in eyewitness identification. *Journal of Applied Psychology, 63,* 345-351.

Loftus, E. F. (1979). *Eyewitness testimony.* Cambridge, MA: Harvard University Press.

Loftus, E. F., Miller, D. G., & Burns, H. J. (1978). Semantic integration of verbal information into visual memory. *Journal of Experimental Psychology, Human Learning, and Memory, 4,* 19-31.

Logan, A. (1970). *Against the evidence: The Becker-Rosenthal affair.* New York: McCall.

Luce, T. S. (1974). Blacks, whites and yellows: They all look alike to me. *Psychology Today, 8,* 106-108.

Malpass, R. S., & Kravitz, J. (1969). Recognition of faces of own and other races. *Journal of Personality and Social Psychology, 13,* 330-334.

Markman, S. J., & Cassell, P. G. (1988). Protecting the innocent: A response to the Bedau-Radelet study. *Stanford Law Review, 41,* 121-160.

Matzner, D., & English, M. (1973). *Victims of justice.* New York: Atheneum.

Monday finally comes for weekend killer. (1982, August 15). *Houston Chronicle,* p. 1.

Morris, E. (Director). (1988). *The thin blue line* [Film]. New York: Miramax Films.

Ohio doctor accused of 36 rapes: Man jailed for two of them is freed. (1982, September 24). *New York Times.*

Olsen, J. (1991). *Predator: Rape, madness, and injustice in Seattle.* New York: Dell/Baantam.

Packer, H. (1968). *The limits of the criminal sanction.* Stanford, CA: Stanford University Press.

Peters, T. J., & Waterman, R. H., Jr. (1982). *In search of excellence: Lessons from America's best-run companies.* New York: Harper & Row.

Prosecution style blamed in flawed cases. (1989, April 16). *Dallas Morning News,* pp. 31A-32A, 39A.

Radelet, M. L., & Bedau, H. G. (1992). *In spite of innocence: Erroneous convictions in capital cases.* Boston: Northeastern University Press.

Radin, E. (1964). *The innocents.* New York: William Morrow.

Rattner, A. (1983). *When justice goes wrong: Convicting the innocent.* Unpublished doctoral dissertation, Ohio State University.

Rattner, A., Weimann, G., & Fishman, G. (1987). *Cross-ethnic identification and misidentification.* Unpublished manuscript.

Reik, T. (1959). *The compulsion to confess.* New York: Farrar, Straus & Cudahy.

Rosen, S. K. (1976). Compensating the innocent accused. *Ohio State Law Journal, 37,* 705-728.

Rutherford, A. (1984). *Prisons and the process of justice: The reductionist challenge.* London: Heinemann.

Sagarin, E. (1975). *Deviants and deviance: An introduction to the study of disvalued people and behavior.* New York: Praeger.

Schein, E. H. (1985). *Organizational culture and leadership.* San Francisco: Jossey-Bass.

Seelman, V. (1940). The influence of attitudes upon the remembering of pictorial material. *Archives of Psychology, 36,* 258-270.

Shapiro, N. P., & Penrod, S. (1986). Meta analysis of facial identification studies. *Psychological Bulletin, 100*(2), 139-156.

Shoemaker, D. J., South, D. R., & Lowe, J. (1973). Facial stereotypes of deviants and judgment of guilt or innocence. *Social Forces, 51,* 427-433.

Silberman, C. (1980). *Criminal violence, criminal justice.* New York: Random House.

16 years in jail, case dismissed. (1983, August 31). *Atlanta Constitution,* p. 1A.

Sobel, N. R. (1982). *Eyewitness identification: Legal and practical problems.* New York: Clark Boardman.

Solzhenitsyn, A. I. (1973). *The gulag archipelago.* New York: Harper & Row.

Some doubt has been raised. (1983, December 26). *Time.*

Teicholz, T. (1990). *Ivan the Terrible.* London: Futura.

Tuchman, B. W. (1962). *The proud tower: A portrait of the world before the war, 1890-1914.* New York: Macmillan.

U.S. Department of Justice, Bureau of Justice Statistics. (1995). *Sourcebook of criminal justice statistics, 1994.* Washington, DC: Government Printing Office.

U.S. Department of Justice, Bureau of Justice Statistics. (1993). *Drugs, crime, and the justice system.* Washington, DC: Government Printing Office.

Wagenaar, W. A. (1988). *Identifying Ivan.* Cambridge, MA: Harvard University Press.

Wall, P. M. (1965). *Eyewitness identification in criminal cases.* Springfield, IL: Charles C Thomas.

Webb, C. C., & Chapian, M. (1985). *Forgive me.* Old Tappan, NJ: Fleming H. Revell.

When nightmare of false arrest comes true. (1984, December 17). *U.S. News & World Report,* pp. 45-47.

Whipple, G. M. (1909). The observer as reporter: A survey of the psychology of testimony. *Psychological Bulletin, 8,* 307-309.

Woocher, F. D. (1977). Did your eyes deceive you? Expert psychological testimony on the unreliability of eyewitness identification. *Stanford Law Review, 29,* 969-1030.

Wrongful conviction charges haunt Dallas prosecutors. (1989, October 12). *Chicago Tribune,* p. 25A.

Wylie, P. (1955). *A generation of vipers.* New York: Rinehart.

Yant, M. (1991). *Presumed guilty: When innocent people are wrongly convicted.* Buffalo, NY: Prometheus.

Yarmey, A. D. (1979). *The psychology of eyewitness testimony.* New York: Free Press.

Zuccotti, S. (1993). *The Holocaust, the French, and the Jews.* New York: Basic Books.

Cases

Argersinger v. Hamlin, 407 U.S. 25 (1972).
Bennet v. State, 530 S.W.2d 511 (Tenn. 1975).
Blevins v. State, 108 Ga. App. 738, 134 S.E.2d (1963).
Escobedo v. Illinois, 378 U.S. 478 (1964).
Gideon v. Wainwright, 372 U.S. 335 (1963).
Gilbert v. California, 388 U.S. 263 (1967).
Ivan (John) Demjanjuk v. State of Israel, Cr.A. 347/88 (1990).
Jackson v. Fogg, 589 F.2d 108 (2d Cir. 1978).
Kirby v. Illinois, 406 U.S. 682 (1972).
Mapp v. Ohio, 367 U.S. 643 (1961).
Miller v. Pate, 386 U.S. 1 (1967).
Miranda v. Arizona, 384 U.S. 436 (1966).
Nell v. Biggers, 409 U.S. 188 (1972).
O'Neil v. Ohio, Ohio Court of Claims, 81-05750 (1984).
People v. Barad, 362 Ill. 584, 200 N.E. 858 (1936).
People v. Harris, 28 Cal. 3d 935, 623 P.2d 240 (1981).
People v. Johnson, 38 Cal. App. 3d 1, 112 Cal. Rptr. 834 (1974).
People v. Kind, 357 Ill. 133, 191 N.E. 244 (1934).
Powell v. Alabama, 287 U.S. 45 (1932).
Roe v. Wade, 410 U.S. 113 (1973).

Simmons v. United States, 390 U.S. 377 (1968).

State v. Engel, 289 N.W.2d 204 (N.D. 1980).

State v. Landeros, 20 N.J. 76, 118 A.2d 524 (1955).

State of Delaware v. Bernard T. Pagano, Delaware Superior Court, Wilmington (1979).

State of Israel v. Ivan (John) Demjanjuk, Criminal Case No. 383/86 (1986).

Stovall v. Denno, 388 U.S. 293 (1967).

United States v. Ash, 413 U.S. 300 (1973).

United States v. Garsson, 291 F. 646, 649 (S.D. N.Y. 1923).

United States v. Wade 388 U.S. 218 (1967).

United States v. Williams, 592 F.2d. 1277 (5th Cir. 1979).

Index

169

About the Authors

C. Ronald Huff is Director and Professor, School of Public Policy and Management, and Director, Criminal Justice Research Center, at the Ohio State University. He has also held faculty positions at the University of California (Irvine) and Purdue University and served as a visiting professor at the University of Hawaii. His publications include more than 50 journal articles and book chapters and 10 books, the most recent of which, an all-new second edition of *Gangs in America,* will also be published by Sage in 1996. He has served as a consultant on crime and public policy to the U.S. Senate Judiciary Committee, the F.B.I. National Academy, the U.S. Department of Justice, five states, and numerous federal, state, and local organizations. His recent honors include the Donald Cressey Award from the National Council on Crime and Delinquency (1992), the Paul Tappan Award from the Western Society of Criminology (1993), and the Herbert Bloch Award from the American Society of Criminology (1994).

Arye Rattner is Professor of Sociology at the University of Haifa in Israel. He served until recently as Chair of the Department of Sociology and Anthropology at the University of Haifa and has served also as the Chair of the Israel Criminology Council. He has published several articles on wrongful conviction and eyewitness identification and has recently published a number of articles that have dealt with attitudes toward the legal system and have attempted to construct models of legal disobedience. He is currently involved in a research project examining how both Jews and Arabs are processed in the criminal justice system in Israel.

Edward Sagarin (deceased) was Professor of Sociology at City College and City University of New York and also served as Distinguished Visiting Professor of Sociology at the Ohio State University. Prior to his death in 1986, he enjoyed a highly productive career in criminology which was recognized by his peers, who elected him President of the American Society of Criminology and designated him Editor-in-Chief of *Criminology: An Interdisciplinary Journal,* the Society's official journal. He was regarded as an intellectual, a prolific author of books and articles in both criminology and the sociology of deviance, and an outspoken advocate of justice and compassion for those who were disvalued by society. His intellect, energy, and dedication helped inspire many younger scholars, including his coauthors on this volume.